LEADER
NOMICS

LEADER
NOMICS

Life and Leadership Lessons
from My Mentor, Economics

SEUNG PAIK

Linear Press

Published by Linear Press, San Francisco, CA
www.leadernomics.org

Edited and designed by Girl Friday Productions
www.girlfridayproductions.com

Cover design: Kathleen Lynch
Image credits: cover © iStock/Yutthana Gaetgeaw

ISBN (hardcover): 979-8-9928954-2-1
ISBN (paperback): 979-8-9928954-0-7
ISBN (ebook): 979-8-9928954-1-4

Library of Congress Control Number: 2025909092

First edition

CONTENTS

PREFACE

Recall that youthful season of life—finishing high school, maybe college, moving out, and starting that first real job. Gradually, then all at once, we found ourselves riding the roller coaster of adulthood, buckled in by responsibilities and decisions. We encountered new challenges, different environments, changing relationships, and of course all those bills. And that was just the beginning. We yearned to come of age, but quickly discovered the ride wasn't exactly the amusement we had anticipated. Crazy to think how many of these early decisions launched our life trajectory. How did we navigate the twists and turns? Where did we find that trustworthy advice before Google?

Perhaps we relied on a network of family and friends, teachers and coaches, our community of care. But did anyone *really* know us— what we wanted or needed, and what we were going through? *Did we even know ourselves?* Decisions became influenced by misperceptions, undue pressures, private agendas, and everyone's personal baggage. Was anyone's advice truly objective? It was easier and safer to isolate and turn to intuition. As long as the decision felt or seemed right, we could skip over concerns like rationality, scarcity, and tradeoffs and lean completely on our emotional impulses and novice instincts. We relied on wishful thinking and defaulted outcomes to trial and error. And when we were gripped by fear, decisions turned into indecisions either deferred or sucked away by time. If we somehow ended up OK, was that good? Could it have been better? And did we even consider something called best? Prodigal decision-making overflowed, and in hindsight, we were fortunate to survive. *Where was that insightful and objective decision framework?*

Seasons change and lives progress, but does our decision-making?

Ready or not, we enter a heightened stage in which we are now called to lead—at home, in the workplace, and throughout our community. The roller coaster moves faster and drops farther as the tough decisions keep coming. But this time, our choices impact the lives and trajectories of others. We're accountable to teams, to organizations, and to future generations. If our decision-making barely evolves, what can we expect of ourselves as leaders? Many will attempt to ignore or avoid the call to lead, to diminish the role or abdicate it altogether. Others might begrudgingly comply, saying, "I never asked or wanted to lead." And some will pursue leadership but with ulterior motives, perhaps a desire for power and prestige. Is it surprising that so few are humbly postured, ready and eager to answer the call? Sadly, it doesn't matter. Leadership is synonymous with growing up, and at some point, it befalls every person. Whether we acknowledge it or not, the responsibility stands far and above personal desires and individual preferences. There is a season when we need to permanently step up, once and for all, but do we? *Where's that humble, willing, and competent leader?*

It's one thing to excuse prodigal decisions when no one else is affected; it's another to allow prodigal leadership to societally persist. Haven't we all felt the void and concluded, *Enough is enough*? We need mentors to raise sound leaders. But look around. Where do we see organic relationships developing between mentors and protégés? Do they exist, and are they a priority? We'd like to assume they're happening across every social sphere. And no doubt, mentorship has been a long-established practice within certain professions like the military and in corporate America. But even there, is it *actually* happening and consistently ongoing? If not formally, at least informally? If the call to lead is falling on deaf ears and unqualified hearts, perhaps mentorship has become the greatest void, and the vacuum we see in leadership is merely the reflection. *Mentorship, then, can no longer be assumed, but it too must be groomed.* After all, is it natural to proactively engage with another in sincerity and authenticity? To carve a clear path forward from past experience? To be objective yet sympathetic? Is it natural to be able to gently probe the thoughts and intentions of others without judgment? To exemplify transparency and vulnerability? And to speak the truth with compassion but without compromise? Is any of this natural? *Mentorship needs to be mentored.* Mentors of all people should seek continuous wisdom and refinement to valiantly shepherd young leaders. These three things—decision-making, leadership, and mentorship—must not be left wandering as the wayward trilogy.

But alas, awaiting at every stage and season of life, full of patience and hope, there stands a universal mentor calling out to every prodigal: "Decision-maker, leader, mentor—are you ready to come home?"

INTRODUCTION

"They're going to eat you alive!" My physics teacher was fed up. Senioritis had set in, and I was again late to class. I had been accepted to the United States Air Force Academy, and my teacher decided a few words of "encouragement" were in order. Only months prior, the Academy was nowhere on my radar. Unbeknownst to me, our high school gymnastics coach sent a performance video to the military service academies, and the Air Force was the first to reach out. My dad, sort of a history buff, was the most excited. He knew of the service academies and held America's military in the highest regard. Dad's first encounter with those in uniform was inside a refugee camp. At age twelve, he and his older brother fled North Korea, believing the rest of their family would soon follow. But they never did. It would be their last time together. From a place of war-torn loss and sorrow, Dad fondly remembered the American GI. He painted for us the image of gentle, warmhearted soldiers who approached him with kindness and candy. Appearing larger than life, they delivered a tangible sense of hope. With glossy eyes, Dad would always finish the story in his broken, heartfelt words, "I never forget that." And he never has.

Together we decided to fly to Colorado and take a look. Embedded in the foothills of the Rockies, the Academy was breathtaking. It was otherworldly to go from Chicago's suburban strip malls to an evergreen-filled campus overflowing with wild turkeys and deer. I witnessed students marching, planes flying, bugles blowing, and young men and women standing tall, inspired by a deeper purpose. *What kind of strange utopia is this?* While we were traveling back to

Chicago, Dad asked with anticipation, "What did you think?" I had to admit, it was pretty impressive. It checked all the right boxes. Great academics, state-of-the-art facilities, Division 1 gymnastics, and well respected. Perhaps most important, it was "free," 100 percent government funded. With two sisters in college and parents knee-deep in loans, the decision appeared to be a no-brainer. And of course, it made Dad happy.

Off I went, into the wild blue yonder. Hot on the heels of *Top Gun*, every cadet seemed fixated on being the next Maverick. Everyone except me. I had terrible vision, and even the calmest of commercial flights made me sick. My Honduran roommate was the exact opposite. He'd dreamed of attending the Academy since he was a young child, and military life was in his blood. His father had flown fighters for the Honduran Air Force, and he was destined to follow. I'll never forget the look of disappointment when he enthusiastically asked which jet I most wanted to fly, and I responded in the negative. You could hear his bubble burst. But he remained undeterred: "Who or what inspired you to pursue the Air Force and the military?" Nothing, really. I had no personal convictions other than Dad's story, but it wasn't *my* story. Alas, my roommate asked the inevitable: "So, what are you doing here?" The checklist suddenly felt shallow and inadequate. My reasons weren't wrong, but they no longer seemed good enough. I wanted to boldly proclaim, "Patriotism!" After all, we did own two American-made cars. But my patriotic vibe went about as deep as a few firecrackers on the Fourth, remembering the Pledge of Allegiance, and listening to the national anthem at ballgames. One thing became clear: "free" wasn't so free. Every predawn wake-up call, followed by endless hazing from upperclassmen, was our daily reminder.

More than producing pilots and military strategists, the service academies were in the business of developing leaders ready to answer our nation's call. *But how could I lead in an institution that I had little desire to serve or follow?* I enjoyed freedom's benefits but was hardly willing to bear its sacrifices. My physics teacher had me pegged. The hypocrisy was *eating me alive*. The longer I stayed, the more I felt like a fraud. Yet, the more I invested, the more entrenched I became. Confusion turned into a crisis of decision-making, character, and leadership. *How can I quit now? Where would I go? What would I do? And what would others think?* I desperately needed a guide. But who could it be, when everyone was marching to the same beat?

—

Year two at the Academy began. In the classroom, I was met by a professor wildly waving his arms and moving his body in a contorted flow. Referencing the awkward movements, he asked, "What's the purpose of economics?" No one was willing to take a stab at an answer. He raced to the whiteboard, and from one end to the other drew a continuous roller-coaster curve—up, down, all around—mimicking his silly dance. He then placed a large dot somewhat randomly on the curve and finally came to a stop. The professor reengaged. "If you have no response for econ, how about the purpose of the first derivative in calculus?" With calculus having been a prerequisite, several students confidently chimed in: "To find the slope at any point on a curve."

"Exactly." Returning to the board, the professor illustrated the slope by drawing a straight line through the dot, skimming the curve's surface. Resuming his dance, he reached a crescendo with this manifesto: "Econ is filled with calculus because you'll see that the purpose of econ is to take this roller-coaster, confusing, complex, chaotic, uncertain, emotion-filled world, and . . . BOOM! . . . make it linear." At "boom," he ceased all motion and emphatically extended his right arm across his body, matching the straight line on the board. Calmly, he then concluded, "In every season of life, at any given point, this is what we need. We need a framework to see more clearly, to think more simply, to decide more confidently, and to lead more courageously. We need linear. This is the purpose of econ." The clouds rolled back and the seas parted. Standing before me was my guide. And I wasn't talking about the dancing professor, although he was pretty good. It was econ. *You had me at "linear."*

Lesson by lesson, principle by principle, truth and direction unfolded. Economics revealed preferences and values. (How did it know me?) Econ opened my eyes to my blind spots, aversions, and fears. (How was it able to see into the hidden parts?) Econ nudged me to balance, prioritize, and grow in discipline. (How did it hold me accountable?) And it challenged me to never settle, but to seek the greatest joys and benefits. No one cared more about my scarce resources, avoiding future regrets, and eliminating unworthy costs than econ. But the question remained: *Should I stay or should I go?* Two years were now invested in my Academy journey, but this unfolding revealed a clear and present decision. I needed to see just how green the grass was on the other side and to reexamine the costly sacrifice involved with military service. If I was ever going to fulfill the Academy's mandate to lead with integrity, I had to be led by personal conviction.

So, I removed the uniform and opted for stop-out, a gap year sanctioned by the Air Force. If I chose not to return, there would be no strings attached. I transferred to the University of Illinois, and at first glance the grass was indeed vividly green. It felt amazing to be "normal," to be back among my high school friends, and to experience the newfound freedom of college life. Hazing and predawn wake-up calls were replaced by late-night parties and "optional" classes, and pajamas became the uniform of the day. Life couldn't have been any more carefree and fun. But the grass withered and the green eventually faded, leaving me with an unexpected, opposing crisis. Pricking at my conscience was that otherworldly place. How many parties and how much fun would it take to outweigh the mission and purpose I left behind? *As with the crisis before, could econ once again guide me through?*

Whether I returned or not, my parents shared how proud they already were that I'd attended the Academy. Dad confessed that my presence there and the privilege to serve our nation was something he vicariously desired. I was reminded that the freedoms and opportunities we enjoyed, and the security Korea needed to rebuild, were made possible by the nearly thirty-seven thousand American lives lost during the Korean War. The Paik family owed an eternal debt of gratitude, and my service represented a little payback for us all. It was then that I realized Dad's story wasn't just his. It was *my* story all along, and that of generations to follow. Having discovered my North Star, I finally had the right box checked: a sense of connection and purpose that far exceeded any bitter cost I'd previously battled. It was the conviction I needed to leave the parties behind and to wholeheartedly return to the Academy—to wear that fondly remembered uniform, bearing patriotism and hope, for the next twenty-five years.

—

Life has a way of coming full circle, and sometimes we get a chance to mentor those whom we once were. A decade after my crisis I had the privilege of teaching economics at the Air Force Academy and stared into an audience all too familiar. As we experienced 9/11 together, my students sat somber, dazed and confused. A chaotic, complex, and uncertain future stood before them—an imminent and towering threat. Textbook graphs and formulas may have checked the academic box but fell short of their attention and far from their affections. It's here that Leadernomics was born. Remembering my wildly animated professor, I departed from tradition and unfolded the core principles with personal stories steeped in miscues and prodigal failure. I dared not hold back the vulnerability, so they too might see econ's insightful transparency, recognize its immediate relevance, and come to embrace the beauty of that same linear framework I so desperately needed. That semester became a memoir for the classroom, weaving together life and leadership lessons as guided by my faithful mentor, economics. Leadership and economics have always been human endeavors, and as a blend of both, Leadernomics aims to inspire every person toward their most worthy investments with the greatest returns.

From self-transformation (chapter 1)

to transforming hearts and minds (chapter 2),

from leaping over fear (chapter 3)

to exceeding individual potential (chapter 4),

from embracing rest (chapter 5)

to building the best (chapter 6),

from fighting victoriously (chapter 7)

to experiencing the unimaginable (chapter 8),

Leadernomics extends values, purpose, and priorities (chapter 9)

by pursuing what should be and never settling for what is (chapter 10).

Life has never made its way off that roller-coaster curve, but econ has at every point steered me clear. It was ready and relevant then and is equal to the task today and tomorrow. My friends, welcome home to Leadernomics!

CHAPTER 1

SUNK COST—LET'S BEGIN BY BURYING

Be ready at any moment to give up what you are for what you might become.

—W. E. B. Du Bois

BLUF (military term for "bottom line up front"): No one enjoys seeing valuable assets go down the drain. Whether it's time, money, energy, or talent, putting to death any significant investment is painful. Yet this is the exact decision we often need to make in order to move forward. It's trading the old for the new, the past for the present, and what was for what could be. To see and seize the opportunities ahead, we must bury the unrecoverable loss that's behind. Our leadership journey begins here, because apart from this, there's little hope of renewal and transformation.

—

"This is the FBI . . . we're trying to reach Seung Paik." The bureau was making its way down a list of customers to warn them. The general contractor I had hired was a fraud. Sadly, the damage was done. Our entire life savings was gone—and that was just the beginning.

SUNK COSTS—A FACT OF LIFE

Think of any valuable expenditure that afterward cannot be recovered. No refund, no exchange, no credit or reimbursement. The cost incurred becomes a thing of the past, a lost investment . . . a sunk cost. Cash placed in a slot machine, win or lose, is the casino's permanent take. The fee charged at an all-you-can-eat buffet is the fixed price of entry, regardless of the quality or quantity of food consumed. The college tuition paid at enrollment is without any provisions for graduating or securing a job. Money aside, consider the irretrievable time, effort, and emotions invested in relationships, careers, and lifelong hobbies and passions. Some professions demand physical assets beyond conventional norms, such as the dedicated athlete, actor, or dancer, or those in the business of life, health, and safety—each bears a measure of bodily sacrifice. Then there are expenditures that may not actually be sunk, but due to transaction costs might as well be. Bags full of unused, unreturned items from Home Depot would be a testament to that, as would my pile of undisputed parking tickets in San Francisco. Perhaps not sunk by definition but cost prohibitive to pursue. However mundane or profound, sunk costs are everywhere, knocking. They're life's continuous price of admission.

THE FALLACY AND ITS POWER

For lesser matters, "It is what it is" ought to be sunk costs' recurring mantra. They may grab our attention for a moment, but the pace of life with its many decisions should repeatedly suggest that we accept these costs and move on regardless of their redeeming value. Eating continuously at the buffet may temporarily assuage our "get my money's worth" psyches, but that doesn't lessen the fixed expense. It's a lesson we should learn to apply early and often. *Yet when our valuable sacrifices and the loss of our precious assets reach a painful threshold, when our lofty expectations appear to have found total waste, the reality of unrecoverable loss strikes an arresting nerve.* What's been sunk no longer seems an acceptable fact of life, but an immovable and twisted anchor upon our rational core. Herein lies the fallacy's opportune moment. In our failed and vulnerable state, the ghost of investment past subtly whispers, "Don't bury me, I'm not dead yet." The fallacy convinces us that, with added persistence, whatever is sunk may still be rescued. *Place one more bet and make back the prior loss. Double down on that beaten-down stock and accelerate the chance of breaking even.* The fallacy holds true for more than just financial investments. Consider underwhelming relationships, jobs, college majors, business strategies, and even political positions. We hold fast to the status quo, clinging to the notion that somehow things will improve. The fallacy plays to our emotions and pragmatism. It knows our aversion to loss and empathizes with our many regrets. Though illusory, the fallacy holds the glimmer of hope we so desperately desire. *After all, we've invested so much.*

Do we recognize the fallacy? Do we hear its persuasive voice? When we keep sunk costs alive and allow unrecoverable loss to linger, we're inviting the fallacy to enter. Instead of cutting our losses and making subsequent decisions based on their own merit, our rational lens becomes clouded by all that's behind, eclipsing our ability to focus on what's truly relevant. When this happens, irrationality doesn't just knock but seeks to devour.

—

It was a hot summer evening when the FBI called. Married with two children and our third on the way, I was twelve years into my Air Force career. We were living in DC and I was stationed at the Pentagon, the Super Bowl for those in my line of work. The hours were long but rewarding, and I was in a proud season of life personally and professionally. It was also a time of exuberant expectations across America's housing market, and we had finally saved enough to join the party. My wife called me at work, excited about the inside tip she'd heard about a two-bedroom bungalow in our favorite neighborhood. It seemed unimaginable that a tiny fixer-upper with pink shag carpeting could fetch half a million, but the property was a bargain for that area. Fearing a bidding war, we preempted the open house and made an offer well above asking. The seller accepted! A few months later at our local mall, we saw a kiosk displaying the "before and after" pictures of beautifully remodeled homes. I called the number on the brochure, and the very next day I received a visit from the contractor himself. He was an older gentleman with a gray beard and was wearing reading glasses. Alongside him was his wife. She was much younger than him and was energetic and kind, especially toward our children. With measuring tape in hand, they walked every inch of the house, jotting down copious notes. The two were a winsome couple, and my wife and I felt an instant connection. Without hesitation, we signed the contract and paid a third up front. Crews arrived and the demo began. Debris mounted quickly as the house became a gutted disaster zone. As for the pink shag carpeting? Never to be seen again. It was exhilarating. I happily cut another check as we ordered new flooring and appliances. Overnight, our family routine flipped. Meals were eaten out, cleaning dust became a nightly task, and without a water heater, the kids' bath time consisted of a cold dip and rinse. We were exhausted, but the sacrifice would soon be worth it. With items on order, we cherished a few weeks of calm before the next storm. But then came the call: "Mr. Paik, we've been trying to reach you. Your contractor . . . he's a fraud." The FBI had been tracking him for over two years under several aliases. What started as a legitimate, licensed business had become a coverup for debts, gambling, and drugs.

Me: You must have the wrong person. Our contractor is a husband-and-wife team.

FBI: She's involved. Do not give them anything.

Me: I've already written checks for sixty thousand dollars.

FBI: Call your bank and cancel immediately.

Me: What if the checks have cleared?

FBI: Then the money is likely gone.

Me: What do you mean, "The money is gone?"

FBI: Spent or transferred. They're on the run.

I couldn't believe what I was hearing. I hung up the phone and immediately dialed the husband-and-wife team. No one picked up, and their voicemail was full. The next morning, I called my bank, and they confirmed that the checks had cleared. I contacted the appliance and flooring stores and was told they had not been paid. And as for our new heating system, no order had been placed. I raced to the mall only to find the kiosk emptied and abandoned. Panic officially set in. How could anyone do such an unconscionable thing? He'd shaken my hand

and given me his word. His wife had held our children. All my years of studying economics taught me that the only thing left to do was to mourn the sunken loss and bury it forever. But how could I? It was our entire life savings. I refused to believe this was the end of the story.

NO ONE IS IMMUNE, BUT SOME ARE PARTICULARLY SUSCEPTIBLE

Sunk costs aren't a matter of if, but of when and how severe. It didn't matter that I preached against the fallacy a thousand times. In fact, claiming to be an expert had me feeling far worse. Human nature yearns to be made whole, to be restored. The fallacy preys on these instinctive desires and the emotions that are tightly wrapped around loss.

The Fallacy Targets Loss's Magnitude

For someone of great wealth, losing $60,000 may have seemed trivial, but for us, it was every dollar we had saved since marriage. We'd placed all our eggs in one basket, and that basket was abruptly and completely stolen. Ours was a home remodel, but it very well could have been a stock market basket, relationship basket, political basket, or career basket. To see an entirety of significant monetary value wiped away with no alternative carried the weight of totality. The magnitude is further exacerbated by that totality's *perceived* worth—a subjective value based on how the assets were derived and their intended use. Both add meaning and gravitas to the loss. More than its monetary value, the $60,000 represented years of diligence, frugality, and sacrifice. It encompassed safety, security, and the culmination of many hopes and dreams. Together, the totality and perceived worth of the sunken loss carried a magnitude that made letting go near impossible.

The Fallacy Targets Loss's Cause

When the cause of loss can be directly attributed to acts of omission or commission, we experience a level of guilt and shame that comes with personal responsibility. The stress of life in DC was exhausting, and being overwhelmed, I dismissed the need for my normal acts of due diligence. In hindsight, it was laughable how I picked a "kiosk" contractor, relying on a single brochure with no references. My busy schedule convinced me to trust hurried instincts over valid research, and rather than question the lack of permits, I celebrated the project's expediency. The contractor may have hijacked our future, but I'd handed it over on complacency's silver platter. Busyness, rushed decisions, and the lack of due diligence left an indelible mark across fallacy's banner. And it read, "My fault, my responsibility to fix."

The Fallacy Targets Loss's Context

Context refers to the confluence of ego, image, and identity, setting the stage for loss's social stigma. It's how we view ourselves and want others to view us. Context gets shaped by a personal narrative and our surrounding community. The personal narrative is something we carefully handcraft to represent our desired self-construct. Built over time, we strive to protect and uphold our reputation and valued credentials. Our content on LinkedIn, our résumés and bios, our academic achievements and professional certifications are all part of the personal narrative. We showcase what we believe others will esteem.

Our surrounding community is represented by our past and present relationships including proximate and remote connections. It starts with our family pedigree and background, where we grew up, and how we were raised. And it includes our closest friends, teammates, and coworkers and colleagues, while extending into our professional networks, business affiliations, and even the influencers and lifestyles we choose to highlight on social media. Each plays a role in how we think, what we believe, and how we behave. They're the spheres of influence that shape our values and convey our identity. It's a community we cherish and dare not disappoint.

As a father, husband, and military official, as a professional financial manager entrusted with billions of taxpayer dollars, and as a teacher and speaker of econ's eternal principles, I had created a context of smarts and self-driven success, professional excellence and family happiness. It was a context in which I had it all and was determined to preserve it. The monetary loss was only part of the devastation. Equally worrisome was what others would think. How would this irresponsible, total loss reflect on me within my esteemed community? Anything less than the appearance of absolute grit and perseverance would undermine the spheres I held most dear. The fear of public humiliation was combatively intertwined with the loss, and there was no way my ego was going to concede sunken defeat to a fraud. *When loss threatens our context, we're sure to find ourselves atop the fallacy's targeted list.* It loves nothing more than a context that stands atop a pedestal, prideful and unsuspecting.

The Fallacy Targets Leaders

Few people have more at stake, greater responsibility, and a higher level of criticism tied to failure than leaders. Our personal and societal construct is one of being in charge, responsible for others and our organizations. We're the risk-takers, the ones pushing the envelope on ideas and transformation, making tough decisions in guiding a vision for tomorrow. Such actions are likely to incur heavy sunk costs, and by capturing the leader, the fallacy will impact all who follow. *As leaders, it's imperative that we wrestle with loss and its implications preemptively.* Do our decisions require us to go "all in"? What alternatives exist if things go south? Are we leveraging more than we have? Are our decisions collective or unilateral, where the burden of responsibility falls upon one person? Do we have the time to diligently process decisions? How broad and public is our leadership platform? What are the social norms and pressures surrounding our profession? Do others' perceptions weigh heavily upon us? Do we believe failure will gravely impact our reputation, credibility, and career? These are questions to consider far in advance, not at the time of loss. To be forewarned is to be forearmed.

—

With so much personally at stake, I decided to hire a lawyer. If the FBI couldn't recover my loss, surely our justice system would. I maxed out credit cards and poured the money into legal assistance. More than

$15,000 later, the Alexandria Circuit Court reached a verdict. I won my civil case! The court awarded me full restitution for damages and fees. But two problems remained. The defendant was nowhere to be found, and there was no mechanism to collect. It was left to the plaintiff to enforce the outcome. The court advised a collections attorney, but these lawyers were pricey with no guarantees. So, I researched private investigators and subversively started a search for bounty hunters. More time, money, and effort, but cheaper than another lawyer. I had come this far, $75,000 in the hole, and I couldn't turn back now. With credit card and loan applications in hand, I was ready to dive in further.

INTENTIONS MATTER, BUT SO DO RESOURCES AND THE SUPPORT OF OTHERS

The fallacy is shown by "throwing good money after bad," striving after the unrecoverable. But what if recovering the unrecoverable isn't our intent? Indulge me for a moment. If my "throwing good (money, time, effort, energy, emotions) after bad" had been aimed at pursuing justice and protecting society, then the continuance of loss might be perceived as perfectly rational and justifiable. In other words, our intentions most certainly matter, and to presume fallacy based solely on the lack of results may often be an erroneous assessment, both prejudicial and ill-advised. To further illustrate, consider two scenarios that I call "suffering with the sunk" and "the tipping point of sunk."

Suffering with the Sunk

There are times we sink deeper as a matter of practical necessity. We persist not to reclaim the past or recover a loss, but because we sense there's no immediate, viable alternative under existing constraints. It's what I call "suffering with the sunk." Without another mode of transportation, we spend the minimum required to keep the lemon running. When there's no time to train someone better, we continue with the existing employee/contractor because it's better than doing without. And we willingly remain with that miserable job (or boss) because we absolutely need the healthcare benefits. It may be BAND-AIDs on top of BAND-AIDs, but what else can we do when we've run out of stitches? Under the pressures of scarcity, we continue to expend what little good we have in order to gain whatever repairable or salvage value we must. The course of action is less than favorable, but it's not motivated by fallacy. The goal is to survive until the next day. It's not irrational; it's imperative. Hiring a lawyer and then a private investigator could have been my emergency BAND-AIDs if in fact there was no other way to get back on our "housing feet."

The Tipping Point of Sunk

For many of life's greatest endeavors, we need persistent investment to arrive at the tipping point of success. Consider all the passions and dreams we've followed with countless bumps along the road, the skills and talents we've tried to master, the start-ups we've worked so hard to grow, the convictions for which we've campaigned door-to-door, hoping to turn momentum's corner. Every investment we make, though independently sunk, contributes to the cumulative weight necessary to eventually tip the scale in our favor. The problem is that we don't know if or when that might occur, and to stop for any duration could prematurely or permanently debilitate forward progress. Take an aspiring athlete who invests years to achieve the professional level. The journey is filled with disappointments, injuries, and doubts; it often becomes difficult to see the upward trajectory. Until one day, the athlete's perseverance is rewarded. They reach that elusive tipping point, that big breakthrough where their collective investment pays off. The athlete's uphill struggle finally becomes downhill exhilaration, and perceptions of failure are replaced with praise for never surrendering their dreams. If the athlete had quit prematurely, could we definitively claim that they quit too soon? Alternatively, if they never experienced their desired success, would it be accurate to claim that it was a fallacy's journey all along? We'll never know. Though my situation appeared bleak, I may very well have been at the tipping point of success with a collections attorney or private detective—quitting may have been premature. But if I continued and things never materialized, would it be accurate to presume my journey was fallacy? Hindsight's twenty-twenty, but our present decisions carry a measure of mystery for which we must allow grace and the room for other factors to help us decide.

In both scenarios, "suffering with the sunk" and "the tipping point of sunk," our intentions may alter fallacy's equation. But there is a more objective breaking point we must consider, and that's capability—the resources and moral support that accompany our intentions. When our sunken behavior follows "good" intentions but has dwindled in resources and moral support, the fallacy may be more at play than we realize. It's here that the virtues of persistence and determination must be checked and challenged. Even the best of intentions can be deceptive and find their way to pawnshops in an attempt to leverage more. To recklessly pursue "good" intentions without capability is a fast and slippery slope toward fallacy. It's where suffering and tipping can quickly tumble toward tripping and falling. Intentions are subjective and hang dangerously on the precipice of sunk-cost fallacy. It's here that we most need the wisdom of outside intervention (support) and the clarity of objective metrics (resources) before we unilaterally continue. I, for one, was waning in both yet dangerously persisted.

—

On my way to meet with a private investigator, I had more equity checks in hand. My wife caught me at the door and inquired where I was going. Sleep deprived, I had completely forgotten it was a Saturday. Before I could take another step, she firmly held my hands, placed them on her nine-month-pregnant belly, and gently said, "Let it go." I was running late and too preoccupied to listen. She said it again but with greater force: "Let it go!" Confused, I responded, "What do you mean, 'Let it go'?" "Seung, you heard the FBI. They're fugitives. The money is gone. We paid a lawyer and won in court, but still nothing. How are we able to afford investigators when we have no heat in the house? The baby is due any day. Let it go."

FALLACY'S VICTIMS HAVE A CLEAR AND OBSERVABLE PROFILE

The victim's profile—including that of yours truly—is marked by three telltale signs: fixation, deprivation, and isolation.

Fixation on the Past Is the Inability to Shake Prior Losses and Is Defiant About Their Recovery

It may be characterized as preoccupied, obsessive, even fanatical. Fixation willfully remains in a state of denial regardless of the evidence. It's our shock response to the painful reality of permanent loss, drowning out feedback and refusing to consider change. Clinging tightly to original plans and expectations, fixation is determined to be made whole and ignores even favorable alternatives.

Deprivation Shows Across Mind, Body, and Soul

With sunken loss, self-interrogation can become a form of relentless mental persecution. Blaming ourselves repeatedly for how and where it all went wrong fuels regret, anxiety, and fear. Exhaustively replaying the past and incessantly thinking of ways to resurrect loss can take a severe physical toll. We lose sleep and eat terribly, and fitness is all but forgotten. When habits and overall appearance fall into noticeable disarray, and when dysfunctional patterns arise, that may very well reflect the onset of depression. A desperate soul may try to mask the truth, but what's physically visible usually doesn't lie.

Isolation is the Natural Response

Hiding from the presence of others is a defense mechanism against public guilt and shame. It avoids misperceptions, scrutiny, and judgment. Why burden or involve others when no one will truly understand or be able to help anyway? Yet, isolation is where we're most vulnerable. We carve out space to persist in our fixation, ignoring its effects on others. Extending beyond our means, making false promises, and leveraging resources we can't return are common practices.

No checks and balances are in place because we've isolated ourselves. When I was mired in isolation, the FBI couldn't deter me, the judge wouldn't discourage me, and my lawyer didn't convince me. The more we isolate ourselves, the more we tune out the opinions of others and their offers to help.

This is the victim's profile, and it took intervention to recognize my deprivation, shake my fixation, and pull me out of isolation. In fact, it took an entire community. "Throwing good after bad" may seem obvious until we're buried in it ourselves. Counselors reference the five stages of grief: denial, anger, bargaining, depression, and acceptance. Depending on their magnitude, cause, and context, it may take a while for sunk costs to "sink in" before we arrive at a place of acceptance. In the meantime, the fallacy is hard at work manipulating our intentions and deceiving our hearts. More than just vague introspection, acceptance requires an honest assessment using observable identifiers.

—

I couldn't deny that it was almost winter, the baby was due, and we were still without heat. My wife insisted I ask family members for additional funds to start repairs—no more credit cards and no more leveraging what we didn't have. This meant exposing my shame to others, yet that was the first step toward burying my pride, my ego, and my destructive self-reliance. It meant coming out of isolation and shining a bright light on what had occurred. With each funeral procession for my self-image, the fallacy began to unravel. Humility needed to precede the greater good. Finally seeing the fallacy for what it was took the larger reminder that a far better purpose awaited me.

SHIFTING BEYOND SUNK: MAKING IT TO THE OTHER SIDE OF FALLACY

I wish I could say that I was striving for a far greater purpose than recovering my loss. But that would be a lie. It was all about the money and shame. If we can move past the fallacy and gain a larger perspective on what a "win" is, we may stop the suffering and shift away from falling into more destruction. The fallacy's appetite is never satisfied, but a renewed focus can bear fruit in ways and seasons beyond measure or comprehension. *We must remember that, in the end, sunk-cost fallacy is a mirage that derives power from seductive lies and our emotional, irrational inclination to believe them.* To make our way from such depths, to shift our profile from victim to victor, we require the one weapon that vanquishes every fallacy: We need *truth* to make it to the other side. Our susceptibility to fallacy depends on the magnitude, cause, and context of our loss. Therefore, we need to implement measures that will help mitigate these variables. Following are four preemptive actions we can take to loosen loss's grip.

Do Your Due Diligence

Before we decide on that next big investment, we must go through the proper available checks. We may not be able to avoid all the pitfalls or find perfect information, but making the effort to know the knowable is worth the rigor. We should consider the moral support and material resources available to us and make sure both are on board. At a minimum, it will serve our conscience well and help protect our credibility. We must be stewards of our past experiences, reflecting on past sunk-cost failures and revisiting the lessons learned. Just as students review old tests before final exams and athletes study film before the next game, leaders must visualize, role-play, and prepare for contingencies in advance. This is how we keep from repeating the same sunk-cost mistakes.

Create a Culture of Transparency and Vulnerability

Leaders should establish a recurring forum to discuss and exchange sunk-cost scenarios and areas of potential failure. Whether the loss involved capital investments, strategies, or policies, how did others handle their sunk-cost fallacy? Where did they fail and why? What kept people strung along and why wouldn't they break away? Sharing stories not only accelerates learning across a broader audience but also helps soften the stigma associated with loss. To hear that others have been there, done that sets the tone for transparency and vulnerability. And it provides the freedom, courage, and humility needed to prioritize team over individual egos.

Assume the Investment Will Be Forever Sunk

This advice isn't meant to discourage risks or instill pessimism, but it makes room for worst-case scenarios and accelerates contingency planning. As the saying goes, "Hope for the best, but plan for the worst." Assuming the worst lessens the severity of magnitude by helping us prerelease, mentally and emotionally, what we may be holding too near and dear. For example, when we loan money to our family and friends, it's best not to expect anything in return. It keeps our expectations at bay so as not to compound any denial and disappointment, and a pursuit that could end a relationship.

Establish Limits

My wife and I have a steady rule when dining out: If the meal isn't up to par, make it known within the first two bites. That helps us change course in a timely manner before settling with sunken regret. We apply a similar rule before binging on Netflix, so as not to prolong the misery. Establishing monetary limits may be as simple as deciding on a set amount of cash to take to the casino and leaving behind debit and credit cards. It could be setting bank alerts to automatically halt transactions once a certain threshold is reached. We may also commit to time limits to pause, pace, and reconsider. Placing expiration dates on contracts provides space to reassess before renewing or extending; imposing use-it-or-lose-it stipulations (i.e., the leave policy in the military) helps to encourage time off and regulate its request throughout the year; and committing to costly cancellation dates and rules (i.e., certain reservations) incentivizes thoughtful planning and committed decisions so as not to waste valuable resources. Last but not least, implementing performance checkpoints like progress reports, project milestones, and metrics prevents a project from derailing too far before someone notices. Even in trading stocks, we find a stop-loss function to help us automatically exit a falling position. Such indicators provide objective points of action, so we're not overly swayed by our feelings and/or biases at the time of decision. Established limits trigger a strategic pause to stop, breathe, and reassess before going any further.

—

I never did make it to the investigator's office. Nor did I follow up with the bounty hunter. The greater priority became clear: Get heat in the house and prepare for our newborn. Accepting loss was necessary to start achieving a little gain. Burying the sunk meant burying the idols of security and comfort as well as my prideful image. It meant burying the sacred, ego-filled areas that I dreaded burying the most. Quitting the pursuit initially made me feel like a loser, but it was in fact winning. With my tail between my legs, I called Dad in need of money. As I confessed the whole story, I braced myself for the lecture to come . . . but it never came. No words of judgment, criticism, or shame. Instead he said, "Seventy-five thousand dollars? Sounds like a cheap PhD in Life." It must have been the first time I laughed in months. His declarative degree topped every "context" credential I'd previously esteemed, and to this day, for me it's a diploma stamped with humility that sits high above fallacy's banner. In that moment of levity, I was reminded that no sunk-cost circumstance is beyond repair or redemption. This truth was the perspective I needed. And it was just in time. Days later, on October 26, 2004, our third child was born. The sunk cost from fraud hurt deeply, but it wasn't priceless. Our newborn and his healthy presence was. Everything that had been so difficult to bury, that I had been trying to recover for months, paled in comparison to what was now in front of me. My eyes finally shifted, once and for all, away from the sunken past toward that which was present and alive.

CULTIVATE A VICTOR'S PROFILE

Instead of fixation, deprivation, and isolation, the victor's profile is one of focus, discipline, and insulation. Shifting toward these habits doesn't happen overnight, but they are areas we must develop and grow over a lifetime.

Focus on Present Opportunities and Their Future Value

Victors may mourn sunken loss, but they don't linger there. Rather than obsessing over the recovery of any past loss, victors identify the greater goal and focus on that. My wife was dealing with our sunk cost as well, but she didn't fixate on it like I did. That's because her focus was on the present, immediate needs of our family and the future importance of getting heat in the house for our newborn's arrival. Focus rather than fixation allows us to be fluid and able to willingly accept loss, welcome feedback, and receive the facts despite disappointment. For the sake of truth, we must be willing to challenge long-held ideologies, traditions, and presuppositions, shaking stubborn habits and our fixed approach to decisions. Focusing on present and future opportunities frees us to question the status quo and relinquish any loyalties that might hinder us—to institutions, to affiliations, to old partnerships, to prior commitments, and to public statements we otherwise wouldn't retract. Focus doesn't mean "quitters never win and winners never quit." Instead, winners focus on how and when to quit.

Practice the Discipline of Purposeful Self-Deprivation

The victim experiences a deprivation of mind, body, and soul that's damaging. The victor also experiences deprivation, but for them, it's a form of intentional discipline to renew and sustain health. Mental, physical, and spiritual sharpness improves the victor's focus. But this means knowing thyself and adhering to certain practices that help mitigate sunk-cost temptations. It may require undertaking arduous habits and routines, even when inconvenient. To combat fallacy's lies, one area of disciplined self-deprivation deals with social media and its intake. Discipline applies cautionary limits to the quality and quantity of what's consumed so as to protect our time, thoughts, and emotions, and to steer clear of false perceptions. Alternatively, discipline makes time for reading, contemplation, journaling, meditation, and prayer, all of which can have incredible, reinvigorating benefits. Feelings of fear, anxiety, guilt, and shame can be assuaged by incorporating methods that regularly protect and replenish the soul. Purposeful self-deprivation helps us cope with the everyday pitfalls of life. It challenges us to initiate accountability, set milestones to stay the course, measure our progress, and eliminate the downward temptations that surround sunken failure.

Insulate with a Community That Helps Keep Truth In and Lies Out

Insulation calls out isolation for what it is, a false protector. Successful leadership was always meant to be a team sport, leaning on a myriad of trusted advisors in every sphere of life. This is a leader's ultimate hedge of protection. We need to be surrounded by those who can candidly speak into our lives, gently show us our blind spots, and relentlessly warn against impending dangers. Insulation does not mean befriending a group of "yes" people and sympathizers. They may mean well but make matters worse when trying to protect us from hard yet necessary truths. We want to insulate ourselves with bold challengers, those who will esteem truth above all else and speak unreservedly out of care for the individual, family, team, or organization. Good insulators monitor morale and the cultural climate, and regularly question, "What are we overlooking? Where could we do better? What are our shortcomings? Are we persisting in a failed effort with an unsustainable goal? Do we need to change course?" None of these questions is easy when we're confronting prideful leaders with their staunch decisions. It takes courage and integrity on their parts to risk the relationship, and perhaps their career, for the sake of truth, the mission, and the team's overall well-being.

Ultimately, good insulation requires humility in leaders because it means creating a culture where feedback is solicited and people can speak openly, honestly, and constructively without fear of reprisal. It's pride-swallowing for any leader and decision-maker to publicly admit to failure and their need for course correction. Yet if there's a singular key to sunk-cost victory, this is it: traveling the road in community with others.

—

Loss's stigma ended up being a figment of my imagination. I never did face the gossip or embarrassment I expected, but I discovered support that was above and beyond anything I could have imagined. The cause was something that I needed to own but a burden that was meant to be shared. My colleagues were the first responders. They took time to come after work and help me put up drywall, paint, and carry lumber from Home Depot. We scarfed down pizza and drank beers late into the night while talking shop, discussing family, and realizing that we were much more than just colleagues. Our neighbors and church community also rallied around us, providing childcare and countless meals while our house and kitchen were in disrepair. Several local vendors supported us by selling my wife's handmade chalk mats, similar to the ones our kids regularly used when our family dined out. To our amazement, an executive producer from HGTV discovered and loved her products and wanted to feature them on one of their shows just before the holidays. Overnight, online orders went through the roof and we accumulated an amount that exceeded our sunken loss. It took over six months for us to make and deliver the products, but every customer was willing to wait. This was the interest-free "loan" we needed to fix the house. And it launched my wife's brand, Jaq Jaq Bird, now into its twentieth year. Bit by bit, with tons of sweat equity, we finished the renovation ourselves and sold the home at the height of the market, just before the "big short." Not every sunk-cost fallacy has a fairytale ending, but one thing's for certain: The unimaginable is impossible without burying the unrecoverable.

CONCLUSION

What do you need to bury, to let go, to leave behind? The FBI was right. The money was gone. And to this day, the swindlers are still on the run—as reported by the *Washington Post* (2006); *America's Most Wanted* (2008); and CNBC's *American Greed* (2016). Leadernomics begins with sunk cost and its fallacy because it's in our deepest trials—our downward spiral; our powerlessness; our failures, regrets, and entanglements; our desperation and shame—that the greatest potential for transformation exists. Our biggest idol is ourselves, and our toughest battle is overcoming the lies and fears within. Who doesn't fear the onslaught of loss, defeat, and public humiliation, especially in positions of leadership? Sunk costs die hard, thus killing them takes more than willpower. It takes dying to ourselves—our pride and our ego—and it takes a committed community walking alongside in truth. To lead transformation in others, we must first be on that road ourselves. What better way to begin than by burying our sunk costs and their fallacy.

CHAPTER 2

OPPORTUNITY COST—SO WE MAY KEEP OTHERS ALIVE

You never really understand a person until you consider things from his point of view . . . until you climb into his skin and walk around in it.
— Atticus Finch, *To Kill a Mockingbird*

BLUF: Leadernomics begins with two costs, one that needs to be buried so the other may be kept alive. Burying the sunk may ignite transformation, but reviving opportunity cost is what keeps it aflame. It's the lifeblood of thoughtful, considerate leadership. Nothing says "I see you" more sincerely than to recognize another's sacrifice from their vantage point—*their* opportunity cost. This is where we prove selfless authenticity and win hearts and minds.

—

Zero dark thirty, the beginning of another day at the United States Air Force Academy. Each morning started with a monumental decision: "To snooze or not to snooze?" Across the 4,400-cadet student body, I happened to have the lone Marine as my commanding officer. Unlike Jack Nicholson in A Few Good Men, *ours was composed and rational.*

That morning I hit snooze once too often and arrived late to the man-
datory formation. The commander approached, and in his even-keeled
tone said, "Seung, you can sleep in whenever you want, but remember, it
was your choice." Later that day I found posted on my door the formal
disciplinary action, twenty tours. This meant twenty hours of marching
back and forth, rain or shine, in uniform with my rifle. Attached was a
yellow sticky note with the question "Good choice?" The following week-
end I marched, step after step. Unproductive minutes turned into hours
reflecting on what I could have been doing instead. That weekend was
our annual squadron ski trip, but it was now happening without me.
This was the opportunity cost of my decision: the opportunity lost. Was
the extra bit of sleep worth it? The lesson was loud and clear. "No, sir,
not a good choice."

EASY TO OVERLOOK, HARD TO KEEP ALIVE

For every decision there's the value of the next-best realistic alternative, our opportunity cost. It may sound simple enough, until we begin
to break it down.

Next-best refers to the one option we would have otherwise chosen. It's not a collection of alternatives or somewhere in the top ten.
Rather, emphasis is placed on singularity, specificity, and priority. To
say that my next-best alternative to editing this chapter is "relaxing
somewhere" may be accurate, but it's overly general. There are means
and places of relaxation I prefer over others. So, defining *next-best*
takes a bit more rigor. Relaxing by playing a round of golf at TPC
Harding Park in San Francisco? Now *that's* singular and specific.

Realistic warns against exaggeration and falsehood. If I said my
opportunity cost of serving in the Air Force was an NBA career playing for the Chicago Bulls, I would expect you to call my bluff. Wishes
and fantasies may entertain, but they have no realistic value in the discussion. On an exam, I once had a student write that their opportunity
cost of being in class was sunbathing on the beach. But it was winter,
and the nearest warm shore was at least a plane ride away. That earned
a sympathetic D. If instead they had written "an hour nap in the hall-
way," that would have been an easy A.

And then there are flaws in our thinking that muddy the waters. *Multitasking* gives the false impression that nothing or very little is actually being traded off. Waiting in line doesn't feel as bad when your iPhone is fully charged. Heavy traffic is easier to accept when self-driving allows for business calls and a quick shave on the way to work. There's still an opportunity cost at play, but it gets subtly masked by our ability to do several things at once.

Predetermined refers to life's default position—habits, routines, daily chores. Whether it's making the bed, paying the bills, or doing the laundry, we tend to undertake such activities without a second thought. Few consider the opportunities forgone while adhering to predetermined norms. It often takes a major event (e.g., a pandemic, marriage, a newborn) to shake such established priorities.

Present value inflates the value of the here and now and downplays the value of future alternatives. When I was at the Air Force Academy, the immediate bliss of hitting snooze overwhelmed any forthcoming consequences and diminished the anticipatory pleasure of weekend plans. What's visible and tangible gets our attention. That's why we overspend in the face of explicit sales, major markdowns, and outlet discounts. The unseen alternative gets lost in the presence of direct savings at our fingertips.

Fluidity constantly changes the forgone equation. In a dynamic environment, there's no permanency to opportunity cost. The valued alternative can vary radically depending on time, situation, and season of life. At work, the same meeting at 10:00 a.m. on a Tuesday has a completely different complexion at 5:00 p.m. on a Friday, especially before a holiday weekend. And as every parent will attest, getting kids to reserve a Friday night with Mom and Dad is a whole lot easier in their youth than when they become teens. Suddenly they have an opportunity cost that makes family movie night near impossible. Fluidity demands that opportunity cost be regularly revisited to ensure its accuracy.

Intentional neglect implies willful ignorance of the forgone. Not everyone wants to hear the voice of reason, the rational stealer of fun. Adventure seekers want to dive in rather than pausing to contemplate the alternative. If invoking opportunity cost means suppressing spontaneity and killing the thrill of the moment, then some will intentionally choose to forget the forgone.

And last but not least, there's *sunken fallacy*. As we witnessed in the last chapter, it's hard to see and seize another opportunity when we're still fixated on the past and chasing the wind.

—

This list isn't meant to be exhaustive, but to show just how easy it is to misjudge, miscalculate, and bypass the value of life's alternatives. Opportunity costs don't flash in our face or naturally rise to the forefront like monetary costs. Instead we must undertake a search-and-rescue operation—seeking after them with thought and consideration. It requires both mental and heart exertion to keep opportunity costs alive. And as difficult as it is to resuscitate our own, it's that much harder to revive this cost on behalf of others. All this to say, the degree to which we're willing to exert ourselves in this endeavor speaks volumes about our leadership to others—about what and whom we ultimately value.

GETTING IT RIGHT OR WRONG, PART 1: "BRIDGES" AND "TOLLS"

Post 9/11, it seemed everyone in the military was either deployed or supporting those who were. The scene at Charleston Air Force Base, in South Carolina, was no different. It was the primary East Coast hub for air transport into the Middle East, and every member was going above and beyond what was typically required of them. In my organization, airmen outside their deployment window carried double the standard load, covering the work of those gone while sustaining their own responsibilities. Congress had also just confirmed Charleston's designation as a joint base, which meant merging resources and overhead with our neighboring naval station. A good bulk of the administrative work fell squarely on my team. As if all this wasn't enough, I received my own deployment orders to Iraq with only a few months to transition. It felt like the perfect leadership storm.

The year prior, I'd received a godsend for a secretary. She was still relatively new to the base, but her workload quickly piled high. Even so, she possessed an amazingly calm presence toward which everyone gravitated, especially the younger airmen. They would regularly approach her to share their burdens and seek advice, and despite her busy day, she somehow always managed to give them her sincere, undivided attention. She voluntarily joined our early-morning workouts, paid out of pocket to attend recognition ceremonies, and was always first in line to celebrate "her" airmen. She may have been a civilian, but my secretary bled Air Force blue and affectionately became known as the squadron mom. At a heart level she was the eyes and ears of our organization. And for every special occasion, cards would be waiting on my desk, ready to sign and hand-deliver, affording me a commander's personal touch. This was her gift—the ability to see the individual sacrifices being made and then to gently nudge me to recognize it as well. People were paying an enormous price to accomplish our mission, and she made sure I never looked past it.

As my deployment rapidly drew near, the number of loose ends became insurmountable. Buried in the office, I lost sight of everyone's opportunity cost, especially my own—precious final moments with the family. With control over my calendar and purview over every task, my secretary took action. She figured out small but impactful ways to filter the urgent from the important, whether it was meetings, messages, or deadlines. She protected my time and focus, and whatever I left unattended, she promptly distributed to others for assistance. In the most professional and relational way, she conveyed my opportunity cost to others. And sure enough, people responded. It was exactly what I needed before being deployed—peace of mind at work and at home, leaving behind no regrets.

"BRIDGES" KEEP OPPORTUNITY COSTS ALIVE

My secretary was what I call an opportunity cost "bridge." Bridges connect people by reminding them of the sacrifices being made for each other and for their common cause. Her actions spurred support and assistance throughout the organization. Sometimes a bridge can help alleviate the opportunity cost directly, but above all, *bridges serve to tighten the awareness gap between leaders and their people.* In any social sphere, formal or informal, being a bridge starts with seeing and valuing the sacrifice of others, and then having the care and courage to do something about it. A bridge's connective efforts help unify top with bottom and left with right, fostering a climate of mutual respect, appreciation, and consideration.

As opportunity costs are kept alive—seen and heard, understood and shared—we sense that we're not alone, bearing the load ourselves, but that we're in it together, battling and sacrificing for each other and the mission. There are times we may not be able to remove or lessen the burdens, but bonds forged in mutual awareness and sacrifice possess an undeniable strength that enables us to overcome in ways that nothing else could. As leaders we need to develop and encourage more bridges by first becoming one ourselves. It means being a scout, a messenger, and a connector. It means being mindful to pay close attention to the sacrifices being made. And it means taking action to recognize and/or alleviate whenever and wherever we can. It's a special role, but not specially confined to just the "leader." My secretary may have been the lowest in rank, overtasked and underpaid, but boy did she get it right.

—

Shortly before departing for Iraq, I invited Charleston's new base commander, my boss, to meet and greet the team. It was an opportunity to be a bridge for my people. As standard prep, I delivered a list of bullet points highlighting my organization's many accomplishments and sharing a few of the personal sacrifices being made. I had members who disenrolled from classes and placed their education on hold; parents who pulled from their personal savings to cover extended day care; and young families who moved back in with parents and grandparents to receive additional support. Forget about the countless missed dinners, weekends, anniversaries, and birthdays. For loved ones, it was a season of buried expectations and broken promises. And after months of altered lives, an immeasurable price had been paid. Public recognition was long overdue, and this presented a perfect opportunity for the top dog to connect.

As the base commander made the rounds, handshakes and smiles abounded. Taking center stage, the commander voiced gratitude and praise for a job well done. But then there came a comment that deflated everyone: "I know things have been tough, but at least you're not deployed." Did the commander not receive my bullet points? Many team members had just returned from deployment or were on the verge of heading out, yet were still working around the clock. Perhaps they were not presently deployed, but those standing there that day weren't "present" at home either. And in many ways, their proximity made matters worse. It was a comparison that completely missed the mark and shattered the goodness of that moment. To an audience full of weary souls, it was as if their opportunity cost didn't exist, or didn't matter. All I could do was sigh. We knew there was no bad intention, but there was no empathy either. If only the commander had stopped at thank you. Judging by the looks on people's faces, the damage was done. Any possibility of connecting was suddenly lost.

"TOLLS" KEEP OPPORTUNITY COSTS AT "HARM'S BAY"

Here in the Bay Area, it's impossible to get around without the constant reminder of tolls preceding every bridge. And they're not cheap, making us think twice before crossing. When leaders miss the mark with opportunity cost, they exact a prohibitive toll, keeping many at "Harm's Bay." This is the place where people remain unseen and unheard, feeling unappreciated and misunderstood, and their hearts and minds remain distant. People may accomplish the mission and continue to sacrifice out of duty and a loyalty to teammates, but without any connection or sense of devotion to their leadership, it won't be long before that leader's vision and purpose fall on deaf ears. When opportunity costs are kept at bay, suppressed by tolls, they can become a ticking time bomb, as we saw with the Great Resignation and various forms of "quiet quitting." To an outsider, the commander's comment may have seemed harmless, but among those who were heavily burdened, it was the sound of another heartless toll, falling upon pained and sensitive ears. The team remained at Harm's Bay, and despite future attempts to engage them, they never did cross over into that realm of connection. I'm sorry, boss—you may have been the top dog, but you got it wrong.

GETTING IT RIGHT OR WRONG, PART 2: A TALE OF TWO GENERALS

The duality of leadership styles I experienced at the Pentagon proved once and for all that opportunity cost is where hearts and minds are won or lost. Up to this point in my military life, general officers (GOs) were for the history books. I'd witnessed a few here or there, but always from a safe distance. Their platform carried a gravitas far beyond my day-to-day. When I moved to DC, it all changed. I was assigned to an office where interaction with not one, but two GOs became the norm. I didn't realize it at first, but they were a dime a dozen at the Pentagon. Overnight, the mystique wore off and the mythical superhero turned normal human, just wearing a lot of stars. Our office was an intense but intimate work environment. Everyone interacted collegially, including our coleaders, General "Self" and General "Others." They held separate titles and had different responsibilities but were joined together by an integrated mission—develop and present the Air Force program and budget. They had the same rank, same professional development, and similar aeronautical backgrounds. Both had stellar careers and were on track for promotion. Yet the two were worlds apart. The contrast in their leadership perspective and presence was glaring, and over the next year, it proved unmistakable.

GENERAL "SELF"—MISSION FIRST, LEADER ALWAYS

Like the character Kramer in *Seinfeld*, General Self would regularly crash-land into our office. Unannounced, he would head straight for the person with whom he had business. In our time together, not once did he address me by name or inquire about my family. It was always a generic salutation by rank. Not that any of us expected a more personal approach, but in our intimate setting, it seemed odd that it *never* happened. My wife gave birth to our third child during this time frame, but General Self remained completely unaware. Outside our bubble he was articulate and poised, but inside we witnessed Oscar-worthy outbursts. Over time, we became unfazed by the B-grade acting. To his credit, General Self was ultra focused on the mission. He knew how to influence senior officials and navigate the Department of Defense, and was careful to watch his p's and q's with the media. For him, it was about presentation and appearance over substance and content. Rarely did he ask us questions probing historical and analytical depths. Rather, his comments generally centered around how to make the slides our team produced more captivating. To appease General Self's wavering preferences, our office spent hundreds of hours churning products from happy to glad. Except this time, things turned tragically sad.

—

Our team was wrapping up a month-long drill, preparing the GOs for a series of media events. General Self stormed in searching for the project officer in charge of the next day's briefing, and as expected, he wanted to rearrange and "improve" the slides. Nothing complicated, but General Self insisted the work be done by the project officer. Normally we wouldn't have blinked, but this day was the project officer's wedding anniversary, and everyone was aware except General Self. I suppose someone could have spoken up, but with General Self, personal matters were a moot point. We each rushed in to help, but once he locked in, it was over. Looking back, I still regret having failed to do more, to intercede and be a courageous bridge in that moment. He huddled over the project officer's desk, directing change after change, while the rest of us stood idle and helpless. In the end, the outcome was practically the same, but the hours had slipped away. We cringed as the project officer made that fateful call home, anticipating the fallout to follow. You see, his marriage was on the rocks, and every detail for that evening had been orchestrated toward a reconciliation. In our office, canceling family plans was par for the course, but this time we collectively felt his pain. General Self, was it worth it? If only he had known, I thought, surely the outcome would have been different. But then I realized, it wasn't about knowing, it was about whether he cared enough to know. And to that question, we already had our answer.

—

All of life's decisions have a similar "Was it worth it?" competing alternative. But to properly assess this on behalf of others, we must first care enough to know what their "next-best" is. A weekly walk-around, a periodic greeting, a personal question or two might make all the difference in understanding their sacrifice. But traveling this more thoughtful, heartfelt road has its cost. For General Self, this may have meant giving up his personal agenda to hear their needs, periodically letting go of his preferences and daily routine to be more flexible to theirs, altering his business-first approach to become more relational and approachable, and checking his frantic demeanor at the door to be their steady source of calm. Connecting would have meant valuing the opportunity cost of others above his own and bearing a level of personal sacrifice for theirs. That's not easy, but wouldn't it have been worth it? General Self will never know.

GENERAL "OTHERS"—PEOPLE FIRST, MISSION ALWAYS

In direct contrast, General Others was relational from day one. He called us all by name . . . first name. He showed familiarity with our jobs and projects, asking questions involving detail and depth. He was curious about our families and would chat at length about a variety of topics. General Others would frequently come around to ask about our weekend plans or to say thank you in person. There was a spontaneity to his intentionality that accentuated his sincerity. He wanted to know how he could help us do our jobs better, more effectively and efficiently, so we could excel professionally and in our personal lives. Meetings and tasks were streamlined based on these conversations. Like General Self, General Others was mission focused, but his communications were content driven. He asked hard questions that challenged our logic and analysis. We didn't mind late nights when they were centered around substantive tasks that actually mattered. In fact flashy presentations were often scrapped if they distracted from the primary content. No matter the pressures, and there were many, we never saw General Others lose his cool, at least not in public. In our fast-paced, pressured-filled environment, General Others produced no Oscar-worthy drama, but he played a lead role whose character inspired us all.

—

The summer hire program at the Pentagon was filled with talented, ambitious college students. The purpose was to provide future professionals a glimpse into civil service, and to give the government a head start in recruitment. Most interns were assigned administrative tasks and behind-the-scenes grunt work. Nothing glamorous, but an opportunity to network and build their résumé. Ours was a recent college grad—energetic, dedicated, and personable. In her three months on the job, she probably made over a thousand copies and logged more than a hundred miles delivering documents inside the puzzle palace, but always with a smile. For her final day, a few of us planned an informal farewell luncheon. As teammates casually trickled in, we heard a loud "Ahem" from the back of the room. A teammate was alerting us of a special but "uninvited" guest. Standing near the doorway was none other than General Others. With all eyes now staring at him, he broke the silence with a tone of disappointment: "Why wasn't I invited?" We were speechless. While we were fumbling for words, the general continued: "Someone's in serious trouble." But this time he couldn't hide his grin. We all shared a good laugh, but no one doubted his sincerity about the invite, or lack thereof. General Others stayed only for a little while, but before departing, he shared his own personal send-off. Not only did he address our summer hire by name, but he knew her fiancé's name and about their upcoming wedding plans. Her tasks were menial, but General Others masterfully tied her work to the overall importance of the Air Force mission. As he spoke, her face glowed. She felt known, appreciated, and valued. This was his leadership gift—as someone in the highest position, he personally took notice of and esteemed the lowest

*among us. We all knew how busy he was and the value of his time. Yet
there he was, fully present to invest in a temporary summer hire. After
he departed, everyone proudly claimed, "That's my general!"*

—

More than a tale of two generals, it was the tale of two leadership per-
spectives. One epitomized "People First, Mission Always." The other
conveyed "Mission First, Leader Always." Perspective changed everything about their respective postures and approaches toward others:
other-minded versus self-centered, relational versus transactional,
sincere versus superficial, substance-driven versus appearance-driven,
servant-leader versus leading to be served. We all valued the opportunity cost of both our generals—their precious time and energy amid
competing demands. But only one general demonstrated how much
he valued ours.

CONNECTING BY RELATIONSHIP—AN INQUISITIVE, HEARTFELT APPROACH

Before I continue boasting about "my" general, let's revisit the bridge.
As general officers, Self and Others both carried a robust support staff.
Each staff was organized to focus and deliver on their general's respective priorities and preferences. Perspective not only determined the
leader's posture and approach, but it also guided the direction and uti-
lization of their staff. General Self created a pathway that was littered
with tolls, while General Others developed a network of bridges. The
former used his staff as a gatekeeper to keep "distractions" at bay—he
was formal, scrutinizing, intimidating, and unapproachable. The latter
engaged and challenged his staff to find ways to create more connection points, such as scheduling walk-arounds, collecting personal bios
and significant dates, and making the front office a welcoming and
hospitable environment. Each staff adopted their general's persona,
and the difference was palpable. General Others having the where-
withal to pop in at just the right time with just the right information
wasn't solely his doing or done by happenstance. It was the result of

a situationally aware staff that was encouraged to be like-minded—other-minded. General Others may have had incredible capacity, but it was enlarged by a staff he'd empowered to build bridges, remove tolls, and contribute to connection.

Now about those walk-arounds—they may have seemed spontaneous and informal, but they were packed with intent. Listen to the questions General Others regularly asked:

- How can I help you achieve your goals?
- How might I best support your career path?
- If we had extra resources, where would you recommend we invest?
- What can I do to help make your day more productive and efficient?
- Is there anything you need me to convey to our partners and customers?
- What distractions can I help remove?
- Is my front office providing what you need?
- How can I best protect your time?
- What can I do to improve your quality of life at work and at home?

It takes active, intentional engagement to revive opportunity costs. Walking around with a checklist of thoughtful questions was a great start. But over time, the practice would have lost its sincerity if it had not been coupled with action. All of us can follow a checklist, but not many of us will follow up with an answer. If we're going to ask for inputs, we'd better be prepared to deliver outputs. I couldn't help but notice how often General Others would jot down notes as we responded to his questions. And if it was not him, he had his exec walking alongside to handle it for him, again utilizing his staff to be a connector. But most important, if we provided inputs, he provided follow-up.

Conveying selfless authenticity requires an inquisitive but convicted approach. Mental exertion may expand awareness, but it's best served when accompanied by heart exertion—care, compassion, empathy—the conviction needed to initiate and sustain action. It takes heart to listen with the intent to understand. It takes heart to empathize with someone, to be willing to "climb into their skin and walk around in it." And it takes heart to follow up and follow through. Here's a confession regarding one of my pet peeves—people saying they'll pray for me, but then forgetting to do so. It's patronizing. I may not be able to prove it, but I can sense it because *they never follow up.* Shamefully, in my walk of faith, I've done the same—hearing others as they pour out their hearts but failing to listen with heart. And consequently, I too forget to follow through. An inquisitive approach is important, but the heart of the matter is vital. To truly demonstrate sincerity toward anyone's opportunity cost, we must be willing to act upon what we know. Heartfelt conviction bears, in part, another's opportunity cost by following up and following through.

If all this seems uncomfortable or outside the conventional lane in your leadership world, welcome to the club. You're not alone. We may not be on the far end of the spectrum with General Self, but we're probably further away from General Others than we ought to be. If so, it may be an area of leadership where, for now, we need to "fake it till we make it." In other words, we may not *feel* like extending our hearts and being transparent with others in the process. And we may not be entirely sincere, but that doesn't mean we shouldn't try. It's in the motions of seeing and caring that we get in the habit of seeing and caring. When we persist in trying, our motives often begin to change. Fail as we might, are we at least willing to try? This is a good starting point and an ongoing challenge for heart exertion.

Many will say that this "heart" stuff shouldn't be expected or necessary to be an effective leader. There are times and situations when everything may need to take a back seat to the urgency at hand. But if the situation allows, if the "stuff of personal value" can be factored in and included as a decision priority, not merely as an afterthought, imagine the potential "bridge" impact. Think of the vastly different leadership message it would send and how far it might go in winning hearts and minds, so that people will declare, "That's my leader!" This isn't a call to be "soft" on mission, expectations, and accountability. In fact, that would undermine the very essence of our leadership presence. And many should rightfully question our purpose and professionalism as leaders if we were. By relationship, I'm not talking about making friends, though that may be a natural by-product. Instead it's about making an "I see you" connection, seeing and being seen, and crossing the opportunity cost bridge together. There's nothing wrong with us sincerely asking our people how they're doing, and our people asking us, "Boss, how are you doing?" We don't have to ask about weekend plans or intrude into the privacy of one's family, and we definitely don't need to get all sentimental. But sometimes, the very basics of being personal and vulnerable may be the most critical and insightful segue to the professional. Ultimately, we want to know and address the variables that effectively matter most, giving our people the greatest opportunity to holistically succeed. When they do, we too succeed.

FLIPPING THE CHART: "OUR" GENERAL

On the Others versus Self spectrum, where do most leaders reside and why? Military organizations live and die by their organizational charts. These illustrate the chain of command and lines of responsibility, lines of communication, roles and relationships. An org chart provides order, logic, and flow in serving and supporting the leader's vision and mission. In the images below, the left chart is the standard. The tip of the triangle represents the highest position, and its base represents the lowest in the given structure. From the bottom up, everyone plays their part in serving and supporting the direction coming from the level above, all the way to the top.

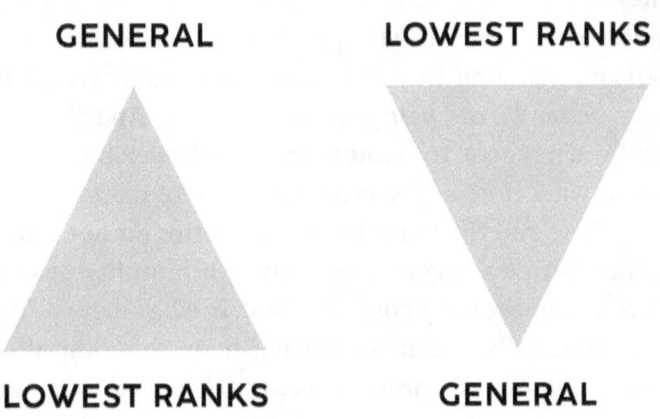

The problem occurs when everything is perceived and prioritized according to this traditional chart, including values, sacrifice, and dignity. We need to reset leadership perspective by flipping the chart. The leader on the right humbly assumes that place on the bottom, as the servant of all. It's a mindset and a heart-set that no longer seeks to be served, but is called to serve and give sacrificially unto others. When a leader flips the chart, they will invariably seek to understand and esteem the opportunity cost of those above. This was General Others's perspective, and it made all the difference. Because he was "People First," we were "Mission Always." There wasn't a wall that any of us wouldn't have smashed through for "our" general. *When people feel seen and valued by leadership, they feel vested, are happier at work, are more inclined to work hard, and are likely to produce better results.* When leaders embrace the chart on the right, they'll often find a corresponding respect—people honoring and upholding the chart on the left, not out of fear but because of connection and devotion.

GO AHEAD, THROW DOWN THE GAUNTLET

One of the more daunting thoughts that runs through my mind before a speaking engagement is this: *Will our time together be worth the audience's collective opportunity cost?* I see myself at the bottom tip and everyone else up above. They all have a next-best realistic alternative that they sacrificed—to be there listening to me. If it's a workshop or retreat, they may be stuck with me for days! Sensing the gravity of that cost changes my perspective. My opportunity cost now suddenly pales in comparison. Standing there, staring at the audience, I'll think to myself, *This better be the best presentation ever.* And then I'll actually say it: "You're about to witness the best leadership presentation ever, because your time and sacrifice to be here matters." Anything less than my best and they may have been better off not showing up. I say this not out of arrogance, but out of a humility derived from their collective opportunity cost. The best is what they've "paid" for. Maybe not monetarily, but in sacrificing their next-best alternative. Some of them laugh at my promise, some are baffled, and some even heckle. But some sit a little more upright, lean forward, and wonder,

Does he mean business? Because now here is someone who has dared to deliver something of greater worth than anyone's next-best realistic alternative. I've thrown down the gauntlet to let them know "I see you, and I'm mindful of the personal sacrifices you've made to be with me. I value your opportunity cost and I'll do my best to keep it alive." Internalizing this principle pushes me to offer the best, most rewarding leadership experience for the audience, far better than what might have been their "next-best."

CONCLUSION

Whose opportunity cost do you need to resuscitate, to revive, to keep alive? Whose sacrifices are being overlooked? From among the Pentagon colleagues under "our" general, there followed in his footsteps five general officers in the United States Air Force. Out of those under General Self, not one became a general officer, as I recall. (Ironically, guess who later published a book on leadership?) When people believe their opportunity costs are seen and valued, it wins hearts and minds, garners trust and respect, and inspires through a moral authority that's far more influential than any formal authority. Every decision we make reveals a corresponding value statement. It may take a while to convey, but over time, decision after decision, the message will become clear. Will our value statement reveal "bridge" or "toll"? Others or self? Standard or flipped? As our Marine once calmly reminded me, "It's your choice." Make sure it's your best and not next-best.

CHAPTER 3

COMPARATIVE ADVANTAGE— THE GREAT EXCHANGE

If everything seems under control, you're not going fast enough.

—Mario Andretti

BLUF: Comparative advantage believes and invests in everyone's unique, contributory value for the purposes of interdependence and exchange. The greatest results aren't found within anyone's individual greatness or superiority. They come when everyone's collective goodness is empowered and unleashed.

—

My oldest was nine, following along as I cut the lawn. He wanted a part of the action. So I let him bag the clippings, pump the throttle, and help pull the cord. With him standing underneath my arms, we pushed the mower together. He was proud to contribute. The following summer, he asked with hopeful anticipation, "Dad, when can I cut the grass by myself?"

"Mom's worried you'll get hurt," I said. But I was the one worried about his safety, the lawn's appearance, and my time. Ultimately, I

wasn't ready to relinquish the task. I was safer, faster, and better, and therefore I had the absolute advantage. He ran it up the chain. "Mom, I can do it. Dad can do something more important." In those few words, he declared his comparative advantage. No matter my superior grass-cutting skills, there were alternatives that might prove more valuable. The challenge was to look beyond my absolute advantage and compare the opportunity costs at hand—his versus mine. Was there a collective good even better than the individual great? Yes, but it would mean re-linquishing control and letting go of certainty to empower another. How dare my nine-year-old use econ against me! But my objection was over-ruled, and the baton was officially passed.

COMPARATIVE ADVANTAGE: COMPARING THE RIGHT THINGS

If you've ever run a relay, you know that passing the baton is easier said than done. Fumbling the handoff can be disastrous, and withholding it automatically disqualifies the team. It's in mastering the exchange that individuals may experience team greatness and a chance at victory. Recognizing the value of comparative over absolute advantage is the critical first step in passing the baton. As my son said, I could have been doing something else of value that perhaps he and others could not do, if only I had passed the grass cutting to him. If his comparative advantage required learning and doing, mine required teaching and letting go. This is what it meant to pass the baton. I needed to see and believe that our collective goodness could be better than my individual greatness. At the start, his performance may not have been "dad-perfect," but with time and repetition, it gradually became good enough. In exchange for his all-important Saturday-morning cartoons, he contributed toward household chores, gained a lifelong skill, and enjoyed the satisfaction that comes from serving. As for me, in exchange for a "lesser" lawn, I was able to tackle a different, perhaps even more valuable household chore. *Comparative advantage assesses opportunity costs when assigning roles and responsibilities to maximize each person's contributory value.* My wife was right. The collective best for our family was for me to em-brace a bit of comparative mess. It was a win-win.

But there was a deeper, more profound purpose at stake. Far more than improving household productivity, the handoff carried a future value of incomparable worth. *Responsibilities and tasks are means for mentorship and development.* For my son, it was about growing in confidence, overcoming fear, and gaining a sense of service beyond himself. It was about taking a noteworthy step that he could claim was on par with Dad. For me, it was about parental leadership, trusting and loving by letting go of fear and control. It was about empowering another so they might experience the joy of contributory value. What's the relational and inspirational worth of seeing and being seen, needing and being needed, appreciating and being appreciated? A few months later I would deploy to Iraq. I needed someone to take care of my chores around the house, and my son confidently stepped up, having already taken the lawn baton. But there was more. Jogging alongside him as he cycled, I said, "While Dad's away, you'll be the man of the house." I told him to look after his younger siblings and to be a good helper to Mom. He dutifully nodded and, once again, took the baton. And he's never stopped running.

ABSOLUTE ADVANTAGE: THE ABSOLUTE TYRANNY

Sharing was indeed caring, but I'd be lying if I said it was easy letting go. That's always been particularly hard for this type A, micromanaging control freak. And the more important the task, the more difficult letting go is. Despite knowing the freedom and potential gain comparative advantage brings, absolute advantage has a way of maintaining a tyrannical grip. In this respect it's like sunk cost, sucking us back toward fallacy.

The Tyranny of Transition

Transition is rarely seamless. Personnel, roles, responsibilities, and routines may all need to change. I suppose we could dump our responsibilities (and many do), throwing the baton and hoping the recipient will somehow safely catch it and run. But a proper handoff involves shouldering responsibility and delegating. It plans, trains, and remains accountable throughout. Added to this are the concerns and frustrations that follow any learning curve. My son could have gotten hurt and my lawn may have indefinitely been a disaster. Transitioning well takes time and effort, and the more complex the transition, the greater the cost. Absolute advantage insists, "It'll be a lot less painful if we keep things status quo and continue doing it ourselves." And so we do. In waiting for the "perfect" transitional moment—timing, person, situation—we end up holding the baton far too long and often miss the window for exchange. *We must transition to achieve the ideal, not wait till the ideal is achieved.*

The Tyranny of the Urgent

In situations where no comparable substitutes exist and time is of the essence (e.g., life-threatening emergencies), choosing "absolute" may be absolutely necessary—the best performer, the most proficient expert, the top producer. Under crisis, they're often perceived as the last, best hope, and rightfully so. The temptation, however, is to keep running those with the greatest bandwidth without discerning "when to say when." As we'll see in chapter 5, "Diminishing Returns," individual capacities may vary, but everyone still has their limits. Therefore we must regularly ask: How urgent is the urgent, and what crisis is really a crisis? When exceptions become the tyrannical norm, we're bound to run the last, best hope to the ground. Passing the baton requires admitting that most situations aren't as dire as we think.

The Tyranny of Control

To decidedly determine outcomes, it's common to lean toward control. Yet control has an insatiable appetite. The more we have, the more we want and need to "keep things under control." It's why we micromanage. This is the person who thinks that unless they take care of it or completely oversee it, no one else can or will, at least not to their satisfaction. There's no one else as reliable and trustworthy as themselves, and pretty soon no other qualified baton holder exists. Bearing the baton alone may temporarily satisfy a measure of assurance that comes with control, but in the end, it's a road for the self-martyr filled with "woe is me." To choose the path of comparative advantage, we must courageously relinquish control and its false promises. And if we can't, don't worry. Control has a way of eventually losing its control in our dynamic world, one way or the other.

The Tyranny of Fear

This is the desperate cousin of control, worried about failure and its perceived consequences. Control may be demanding and overbearing, but fear is anxiety-filled and always on edge. Control demands "my way," but fear adds "or the highway." It manifests itself particularly in those who base their significance on being needed. At risk is their purpose, relevance, and reputation—perhaps their promotion or job security is on the line. Once the spirit of self-preservation takes precedence, beware. From passive-aggressive behavior to manipulation and threats, fear's mindset is to save oneself regardless of the collateral damage. When a fearful leader feels threatened by the possibility of removal and replacement, don't be surprised to find the baton hidden away from those who might run better.

Herein lies the rub. The more excellent and superior we are at anything, the more likely tyranny is to reign. We fear losing the lofty praises and perceptions that surround our excellence. We try to control whatever's necessary to protect our strict standards. We tend to point out all the urgent concerns and contingencies if excellence is compromised. And we claim that the transition from beginner to expert is too time consuming and cost prohibitive. Even something as minor as lawn cutting provoked a level of tyranny in me. I didn't want to deal with the added mess and work that comes with transition. I didn't have the patience or vision to develop a novice for tomorrow. And I definitely wasn't ready to let go of the certainty of my own outcomes. Whether it's people, companies, or countries, absolute advantage has deceptive, universal appeal. Independence, autonomy, sovereignty; strength, power, authority; security, comfort, predictability—all are promised under the guise of self-reliance. But in reality, it's a house of cards. With absolute advantage, I thought I should and could maintain control, but it was tyranny that took control of me. Let's just say, the apple doesn't fall far from the tree.

LOVE YOU, MOM.
TIME TO TAKE A BREAK

Cafe Express was a mom-and-pop coffee shop in Evanston, Illinois, near the campus of Northwestern University. No frills, no thrills, and before the proliferation of Wi-Fi. You'd walk in and hear the sounds of bebop or classical but always the same playlist. Take a seat among the mismatched tables and chairs spread across the clean checkered floor, and enjoy a perfectly prepared latte from their one-of-a-kind barista. This ordinary coffee shop was made extraordinary by a lady named Sun—my umma. *Despite her broken English, Mom had a warm greeting for every customer. She knew everyone by name—and knew their life story, family, vocation, habits and routine, and of course their regular order. Her memory was second to none. Mom always prepared each request with the highest level of care and precision. My favorite thing to witness was how she operated the espresso machine. It was an old-fashioned Italian beast that sat high atop the rear counter. Mom would step onto a footstool and extend the entire length of her five-foot frame to reach the lever. Grabbing hold, her body weight would then gently help her to descend, slowly squeezing the perfect shot. It was an endearing sight to behold. From her youth, whatever Mom touched exuded excellence and the utmost attention to detail. Whether she was a student at an elite women's university or a well-respected pharmacist in her town, whether filling prescriptions back then or filling espresso orders now, Mom never ceased to do things her A-plus way. Customers appreciated it, but her young employees? Not so much.*

I was in the middle of transitioning from California to my next duty station, a one-year remote assignment to Korea just south of the demilitarized zone (DMZ). Despite its reputation for being one of the more grueling mission locations, I relished the privilege to serve in my birth land. With plenty of leave saved, I mapped out a bucket-list trip that would follow the trails of Lewis and Clark. But just days before my vacation was to begin, Mom called asking if I could rush home to Chicago. My sister, then living in Boston, was about to give birth to her first child, and Mom desired to be by her side. She needed coverage at the café, and so Lewis and Clark would have to wait.

It was straight to barista boot camp. I wasn't surprised to find that Mom had an absolute advantage at pretty much everything. Whether it was making drinks, preparing sandwiches, taking orders, cleaning, or running the register, she did everything better, faster, and more efficiently and effectively than anyone else. It was a standard no one could meet, especially not me, though I kept smiling and nodding to ease her worries. For Mom, it was only her age that finally made the pace feel relentless. Her beloved customers welcomed me with unanimous concern. "We're glad you're here—Sun needs a break." And they were right. Constant turnover, rehiring, and retraining exacerbated Mom's exhaustion and constant sighs. Sadly, she couldn't see how her absolute advantage was killing the comparative. It was time for her to fly, but how would the business survive without the absolute?

ABSOLUTE ADVANTAGE BEARS AN ABSOLUTE COST

Despite Mom's good intentions and the many challenges that come with running a business, the tyranny ultimately came from within. It was in her A-plus DNA. The coffee shop was her baby, and she cared for it accordingly. Clinging to her absolute may have felt like the only choice, but it came with a heavy price.

Absolutely Exhausting

Relying heavily on one thing, one person, one resource because they're the best may be OK temporarily, but it's unsustainable in the long run. At some point, fatigue and then failure are bound to set in (see chapter 5, "Diminishing Returns"). Everyone and everything eventually needs a break, some rest and replenishment, and minor maintenance along the way. When there are no suitable backups and no one else to share the burden, exhaustion can spiral quickly—physically, mentally, emotionally.

Absolutely Demoralizing

Persistently doing it all doesn't just stovepipe opportunities, it hijacks them altogether and simultaneously conveys a value message: *Only absolutes are good enough to get it done.* When we don't seek the assistance of others, especially amidst busyness and crisis, we often convey a hurtful assessment, intended or not—that others aren't up to the task, dependable, capable, or helpful when needed most. Or worse, that we don't need them or trust them, and won't miss them when they're gone. *Absolute* carries a tone of arrogance that belittles and pushes away. To withdraw and withhold opportunities, responsibilities, and autonomy are surefire ways to crush morale and leave a trail of disheartened and disinterested souls.

Absolutely Limiting

How often I've heard the expression "The reward for good work is more work." Then what's the punishment for bad work? Is it less work—or no work at all? These are some of the perverse incentives that come into play when we're fixated on absolute productivity and performance. It's not that others can't learn, improve, and contribute, but amid the tyranny, work continually gets transferred and piled onto the few. Such overreliance fosters a culture where the best team members get repeatedly "rewarded" (taxed) with more work and responsibilities, while others remain underwhelmed, underchallenged, and untapped. Instead of maximizing a team's capacity, we drive a larger pool of inexperienced members who will likely be ill-prepared when they're needed to step up. Giving key players all of the keys is a delicate and dangerous place for any team to be.

Absolutely Misleading

Absolute advantage isn't always what we think. It could simply mean that someone stands slightly above in a sea of average. They're the best among a mediocre or weak group. Yet because they're still the "max among the min," more opportunities often come their way. This may be a premature and misleading selection process. When it comes to an unproven, novice crowd—beginners, interns, first-year candidates, apprentices—assessments for advancement should proceed with caution. Early stratifications in any profession may drive investment decisions that overlook mid-to-late bloomers, those who may possess great future potential but are simply slow starters. If we're talking about a developmental group, it may be better to refrain from assessments and widen the investment pool over a longer period to gain a more accurate picture. It's one thing to give opportunity to proven excellence; it's another to rob it from others for those who are unproven or mediocre at best.

Absolutely Discriminating

Sometimes absolute advantage is nothing more than a subjective bias based on variables other than objective performance or merit. One common example comes from youth sports, where coaches are swayed by "absolute" size or strength. It's a visual disparity that naturally accompanies adolescence. Haven't we all witnessed the "big" kid who continually gets the best positions and the most playing time no matter how awkward, out of shape, or slow footed? And if the kid is the coach's child, forget about it—they may never leave the field. They're not the absolute best; they just satisfy the absolute bias. For better or worse, it's a discriminatory practice that starts early in life, where the less developed and the less privileged often get the short end of the stick.

—

Without Mom's absolute presence, we had to survive by committee— me, Dad, my other sister, and the few remaining employees. The abrupt handoff had me fumbling the baton, but we each quickly carved out our comparative roles. From opening to closing, cleaning, and preparing; from ordering and stocking to managing schedules; from handling the register to serving our customers; we situationally, and somewhat naturally, gravitated toward our most efficient and effective tasks and roles. And during the morning and lunch hour rushes, there was no time or capacity for micromanagement. Everyone simply pitched in where they could, filling the gaps, and doing their share. Individually, no one could run Mom's race, but collectively, we moved the baton across the finish line each day. The thing is, Mom trained her employees really well— she just didn't adequately appreciate them, delegate responsibilities and leadership, and entrust them with enough. She was holding the baton too tightly. Few things deliver greater job satisfaction than feeling needed, valued, challenged, and skilled for the fight. Without Mom's presence, a level of tyranny was lifted and replaced by a freedom—to trust, to empower, to think outside the box, to make mistakes, and to have some fun. The employees may not have been paid more, but their tip jar was overflowing. And together, we were more than able to survive.

COMPARATIVE'S CHARACTER

Comparative advantage is marked by dependence rather than self-reliance, and is characterized by humility over individual superiority. It's in the face of limitations that comparative advantage is most needed and embraced. Leaders, our weaknesses, constraints, shortcomings, and frustrations are all meant to serve as reminders for comparative advantage. We don't have to know or do it all. That's not our job. In fact, if we have the time to fulfill the roles and responsibilities of others or that others could do, then we're probably not maximizing our call to lead. Our job is to recognize the potential for comparative advantage in every person, and then to rely on interdependence and exchange, cooperation and collective contribution. Our call is to stare down absolute's tyranny and relinquish its limited, prohibitive powers. Instead of doing more ourselves, we often need to get our absolute selves out of the way to achieve the greatest good. If opportunity cost says "I see you," comparative advantage takes it a step further and says "We need you and value all that you bring to the fight—and with you, we're better."

—

The irony of Cafe Express was always in its name. Under a culture of absolute advantage, the coffee shop could never achieve the "express" needed to survive the industry's competitive and dynamic landscape—not in service, not in ideas, and not in change. It was hard for Mom to let go, but after a few more grandkids, Dad convinced Mom it was time to retire, and they sold the café to Brothers K. Peet's and Starbucks both opened nearby, and rents continued to rise. But the baton had been handed to two young brothers who in practice, if not in theory, understood comparative advantage and were passionate about serving a new generation of customers. Not only did Brothers K survive back then and through the pandemic, but they have since expanded.

The brothers opened another shop called Backlot Coffee, a few miles down the road. It's become Mom and Dad's favorite, and ours as well whenever we visit. When you walk in, one of the brothers is there to greet you, just like Mom used to do. But there's a major difference: He isn't doing it all. In fact, on the surface I'm not sure what he's doing other than smiling, chatting away with customers, and cheering on his team—his comparative advantage. As for the bulk of operations, I see his employees leading, communicating, hustling and bustling, and empowered to fulfill their contributory value. You can see the well-orchestrated exchange across the café and feel the energetic and joyful vibe. A line of customers—young and old, families and friends, students and professionals—all happily await their turn. It's clearly a neighborhood favorite.

On one of our recent visits, the owner walked over with complimentary pastries and coffee and made it a point to personally say thank you to my parents. He shared how much he and his brother appreciated Mom and Dad—that they had never forgotten their kindness during the transition. He recalled how thorough Mom was in her training and that it paved the way for their success. But most of all, he expressed gratitude for trusting them by passing the baton. I think he knew the café was her baby, and to experience the great exchange required a willing handoff from Mom.

LAND OF THE MORNING
"NOT-SO" CALM

From the moment I arrived at my base in Korea, its reputation held true to form. The pace and complexity compressed into one year was uncontrollable, and our Jekyll-and-Hyde commander added to the madness. He could charm top brass with the best of them, but inside our organization he led by fear and intimidation. His constant threat was to replace anyone who couldn't deliver. Thankfully, I inherited a cohesive team willing to cover for one another, including me. Though I was second in command, my boss had a habit of skipping the chain. If I wasn't within eyeshot, he would beeline to my subordinates, interrupting their focus, dumping random tasks, and creating distress and confusion. Being a buffer and running interference became my top priority—and needed to be my comparative advantage.

One of my subordinates was a new lieutenant (LT), less than two years on active duty. The Air Force wasted no time throwing him into the fire. He was the lead analyst for the smallest yet most visible budget on the peninsula, in direct support of a three-star general. My LT may have been young, but what he lacked in experience he more than compensated for through grit, intelligence, and a great sense of humor. He was enthusiastic about his work and a sponge for knowledge. If there was one downside, it was his public speaking. Born and raised in Puerto Rico, he spoke English as his second language. Whenever he became nervous or excited, both his speech and volume would accelerate to new heights. The team found it entertaining, but not our commander.

It was a rare afternoon when I wasn't near my desk. The commander made one of his surprise visits seeking information for our Three-Star. Unable to find me, he grabbed my LT and proceeded straight to the general's conference room. It ended up being an impromptu Q and A session with the general and his entire staff. Later that night I received a call. It was my LT letting me know all that had happened. Ill-prepared and under pressure, he'd quickly grown nervous and begun to crack. His words accelerated, then raced, and then rambled to the point where no one could understand him. The meeting was a complete debacle, and as the two exited the commander turned to him and said, "You're done." My LT nervously asked me, "Captain Paik, what does that mean, I'm 'done?' Am I fired?" I told him not to worry, that everything would be OK. I didn't have the heart to say otherwise. The next morning, I went to the commander's office, and before I could say a word, he confirmed my fear: My LT was indeed fired, and I was to undertake his duties effective immediately.

I pleaded for a second chance—promising that I would work with him on his presentation skills and that it wouldn't happen again. After a lengthy pause, the commander offered a compromise. "OK, but if he screws up, you're fired." Understood.

I didn't share the details of our conversation. I just let my LT know that we'd be ramping up his briefing skills and putting in some late nights. He was relieved, but the team and I faced a much larger consequence: absolute micromanagement. The commander's drop in confidence resulted in more meetings, more interruptions, more scrutiny, and many redundant tasks to double cover the LT's portfolio. We completely lost any sense of autonomy, and the intrusions that had previously annoyed us were nothing in comparison. The next briefing was a month away.

COMPARATIVE'S COMMITMENT

Humility and dependence may be comparative's catalysts, but its defining trait is commitment. There must be a commitment to suppress the tyranny—the urgency, control, and fear. There must be a commitment to transition—to invest in training and to assess relative strengths. There must be a commitment to the future vision—the potential that can only come from collective greatness over anyone's individual goodness. There must be a commitment to support—gaining buy-in from teammates, each committing to their respective supportive roles. And it takes a committed leader—willing to give second chances and having the patience to see the mess through. Getting to a place of comparative exchange and interdependence, contributory value and collective greatness requires sacrificing individual absolute strengths for each other's relative strengths. And that takes the hard work of commitment.

—

When the commander told me that I was next in line to be fired, I'll confess, I wasn't sure what the outcome would be, nor was I certain that I wouldn't regret my promise that my LT wouldn't screw up again later. To be honest, a big part of me wanted to take control, handle the briefings myself, and assign the LT to do something else, something more hidden from the public eye. I didn't know how long it would take to transition his speaking skills, and by now we were under the gun. Besides, public speaking was my strength, so why not just let my absolute advantage take over? It was the assured path, the predictable path, the path to certainty amid the tyranny of urgency and lost autonomy. But it was also the path to a likely future—a future that didn't advance my LT and where the rest of the team would continually be oversaturated. To train, trust, and transition may have required more work in the present (and it did), but developing his comparative advantage offered the greatest collective way forward. Comparative advantage, and not absolute, was the last, best hope for our team's future success. If my LT's comparative advantage required learning and doing, mine required teaching and letting go. So we rolled up our sleeves and committed to the work.

Mock brief after mock brief, day in and day out, we collectively put the LT through the ringer. Everyone observed and critiqued. Demeanor, pace, body language, content, and volume—no public-speaking stone was left unturned. He quickly learned, and I quickly realized that his previous mess was more a result of the baton having been dumped on him. Until now, he had never received any constructive feedback or formal training on how to navigate a budget brief, especially with spears being thrown by senior officials. He was cast into the waves of criticism and threats, forced to sink or swim without a paddle. As a team, we were committed to paddling together not only for his sake, but for ours as well. At the end of the day, no one had better command of his portfolio than he did. Making up the LT's knowledge and covering all his tasks would have taken far more work and long-term effort than spiking our collective efforts for this single month.

—

The weeks flew by as showtime approached. The Three-Star and his staff had convened for their regular update. My commander sat next to the general as I slid to the back, palms sweaty and heart racing. Of all the presentations I had been a part of, none felt as nerve-racking as this. Had we done enough to successfully pass the baton? The briefing started and an hour later, the relay had concluded. The race was over and my LT was on the other side, having taken the baton across the finish line. All I could feel was enormous pride. My LT killed it. It was one of the smoothest, most coherent budget briefings I had ever witnessed. And judging by the look on the general's face, he agreed. Throughout the briefing and into the Q and A, LT's face shone with an almost arrogant, daring look that said, "I dare you to break my confidence; I dare you to ask me something I don't know; I dare you to tell me, 'You're done.'" Every audience member was impressed, and the Three-Star concluded with a word of praise: "Great job, lieutenant. I look forward to the next one." The LT's job was saved, and across the Morning Calm, his contributory value rang loud and clear. My boss was all smiles, receiving handshakes around the room for "his" outstanding mentorship. And that was fine by me—so long as no one was getting fired and we regained our autonomy. It was indeed a great exchange.

COMPARATIVE'S REWARD

Comparative advantage doesn't seek to regain control. In fact it continually seeks to let it go for development, interdependence, and exchange. There's much work and commitment involved, but there's a far greater reward that awaits—the building up of individuals to experience the joy of becoming a team. For leaders, it's not about doing, but about training, guiding, and equipping. It's about assessing, delegating, and entrusting. And it's about encouraging, motivating, and empowering. It's not about casting fear with threats, but about casting a vision for tomorrow and allowing room for growth. In getting our "absolutes" out of the way, we can finally unleash comparative's true potential where individuals shine brightest in the context of team.

—

My LT not only didn't get fired, but he went on to become a senior leader and spokesperson for the Air National Guard—individual goodness now leading team greatness. I recently saw one of his presentations posted on YouTube, and as expected, he's still killing it.

RUNNING WITH DA BULLS

Nothing appreciates diversity and the unique talents and gifts of others more than comparative advantage. Some of us may not have an absolute advantage in anything, but everyone has a comparative advantage in something. We just need to hand off as many opportunities as possible to discover what they are.

—

Hard to believe I've been following the Chicago Bulls for nearly forty years. The nineties were a period of jubilation. It was a dynastic run for the ages. Not one, two, three, four, or five . . . but six championships. Once a game started, no distractions or interruptions were allowed. Just me and the play-by-play announcers. But as with all good things, the Bulls' championship run finally came to an end. And nearly a decade of oblivion followed. It was so bad that I feared another century-long curse like that of our crosstown neighbors, the Chicago Cubs.

But then came decade number three, and the script once again flipped. With the top pick in the 2008 draft, the Bulls were once again relevant and rumbling toward their first title since the Jordan era. The excitement was back, and so were my game-day rituals. Except now there were a couple of distractions sitting next to me, my two boys—Thing One and Thing Two. I was no longer an addict, just a die-hard fan. But these two quickly became Chicago's youngest junkies. During each game, something strange started to happen. Thing Two would start giving the play-by-play, speaking over the actual announcers. As endearing as his seven-year-old voice may have sounded, it was annoying. I wanted the live, real-time broadcast from professional announcers. I wanted the absolute best, not his comparative mess. I could hear Thing One yelling at Thing Two, "Dad said stop talking," but he couldn't be contained. Even with the volume up, his excitement overwhelmed it. What should I do? It was the one team, the one hobby, a decades-long relationship, that I yearned to selfishly enjoy my way.

BEWARE OF ABSOLUTE PARTICULARITIES

Sometimes absolute advantage isn't about an absolute in performance or excellence. Rather, it's about us holding fast to absolute particularities. My Bulls madness probably sounds silly. But don't we all have our list of "absolute" particularities and preferences? How we get things done, our approach, our pet peeves—at work or around the house, alone or with family and friends. They're the tasks and habits that have formed into absolutes. And the manner in which we do things, whether it's excellent or not, we're not inclined to change or compromise, no matter the comparative possibilities. Perhaps it's how we discipline and teach our kids, manage our finances, or lead our teams and companies. Or it could be something less consequential, like how the bed is made, how the laundry gets folded, or how someone prefers to listen to their game. No one is welcome to unilaterally alter things without permission. We have our way of doing things, and unless they're willing to do it the same way, we'd rather they didn't interrupt or bother us. It's once again the tyranny of control, but more subtle because particularities are often excused when they extend into those trivial areas of life. But isn't life full of the trivial? That's where the countless opportunities to pass the baton exist, but we so often miss them. It's in the everyday, practical, and even mundane parts that we must be mindful and most open to the possibility of exchange. The more we're in the habit of passing the baton and being willing to avail ourselves of the help of others, the more we'll begin to experience the contributory value that's possible all around us, in every sphere of life. Relinquishing personal preferences and particularities as opportunities for others carries great potential.

—

I finally decided that whenever a game would come on where I couldn't fully devote my attention—driving, cooking, or cleaning—I would ask Thing Two to give the play-by-play, passing the baton from professional broadcasters to my son. Being encouraged and empowered, he gained confidence and joy. Soon his telecasts became the household norm. The look of his contributory value was similar to the pride worn by Thing

One when he cut the grass. With each broadcast, it became clearer: Thing Two had a gift. As much as I didn't want to admit it at first, he was objectively good. How he had, at such a young age, the ability to simultaneously watch, articulate, and describe every moment of every play was beyond me—he was enthusiastic, informative, detailed, and humorous. Who was this kid? Having handed off this opportunity, I could now see and appreciate his talent. He just needed the opportunity to be unleashed.

COMPARATIVE'S JOY

As I now enter my fourth decade as a fan, I still have Bulls-mania, but one absolute has changed forever. Thing Two's play-by-play is no longer unwanted noise, but welcome in the car, in our home, and at every turn for any and every game. And not just Bulls basketball, but every sport, college and professional. Instead of watching ESPN highlights, my daily fix comes from watching him broadcast live and on air. What once seemed a comparative mess is quickly becoming the absolute best. Silly and trivial? Mundane and unimportant? Passing the baton no matter when or where and no matter how ordinary may be the handoff that ignites an extraordinary passion, leading to unimaginable results. We'll never know till we're willing to release those day-to-day particularities and embrace some of the comparative mess that comes with handing out countless opportunities. And embedded there, somewhere, we may discover the greatest exchange we can make.

CONCLUSION

To whom may you pass that baton, relinquishing preferences, power, and control? Whose contributory value can you empower? Do you see the collective potential? As I stare across the counter, I'm flooded with memories. I met my wife that summer at Cafe Express, and her order was the high-maintenance drink I dreaded. "Double iced mocha, half two-percent, half skim, and easy on the ice, please." I may have been inexperienced, but I aimed to impress. Taming the Italian beast, I finally crafted the perfect pour. The line out the door revealed just how long it took, but she was worth it. I watched her take a sip and then return to the counter. It was "too watery," and was there someone else who could remake it? Oh, the nerve! But most upsetting was that she was right. I had no barista skills to boast of and should have asked my coworker from the start. My comparative advantage was talking to customers, pouring drip, and offering prebaked goods. I should have known back then that she would always be the one who would challenge my tyrannical absolutes, pushing me to pass the baton and empower contributory value in others, especially our children. Though the iced mocha was a flop, something must have caught her eye. I was given a second chance. And twenty-five years later, I now have the comparative advantage in our home. How do I know? Every morning she asks, "Is the coffee ready?" And my tip jar overflows.

CHAPTER 4

MARGINAL ANALYSIS—THE POWER OF THE TWEAK

An object at rest stays at rest . . . unless acted upon by
an external force.

—Newton's first law of motion

BLUF: We've come to our most catalyzing principle. Economics dispels
the notion that to accomplish "big" requires big, and that only big will do.
Rather, we invoke the initiating and sustaining power of the tweak—to
think and act on the margin. To achieve anything, we must first simply
start. One small, incremental step at a time is transformation's surest,
most powerful catalyst. No need to change the world. Just tweak it.

—

*When I was six, my grandfather took me to Wrigley Field to watch my
first Chicago Cubs game. I was hooked. From peewee to high school,
baseball became my obsession. But at fourteen, I was tiny. No coach
would seriously consider this four-foot-ten, ninety-pound frame. I was
cut on day one of freshman tryouts and the field of dreams instantly
vanished. Desperate to fill the void, I considered cross country or wrestling, but one was miserable and the other was brutal.*

During gymnastics, a mandatory PE class, a sophomore on the varsity team came to give an exhibition. But he wasn't just any gymnast. He was the reigning Illinois state champ and already a local legend. From the moment he flew through the air, we all knew we were witnessing greatness. He went on to win several NCAA titles at UCLA, be selected as an all-American and national team member, and compete in the '92 Olympic Games. We all stood mesmerized as he defied the laws of gravity. But what most caught my eye? He too was small. Afterward, I asked how he became so good, hoping it had something to do with our shared size. He smiled. "Lots of practice. You should give it a try." And so I did.

During warm-ups, I watched the varsity team form a circle, and in succession, each did a standing backflip. Arms lifted, head back, knees tucked in, rotating and landing square on their feet. Piece of cake. I went over to a corner mat and did as they did—jumped up with arms lifted and threw my head back, assuming the rest would follow. But my body was suspended in midair and then fell straight down, crashing headfirst. What looked effortless wasn't. Behind the varsity status, there were endless hours of practice and repetitive corrections. As for the future Olympian, he invested more than a decade journeying at the margin: one improvement, one skill, one day at a time. How did I possibly think I could do a backflip on my first try? With a sore neck and bruised ego, I sheepishly crawled away.

MARGINAL ANALYSIS—TO START, SUSTAIN, AND FINISH THE JOURNEY

In economics, marginal analysis assesses the impact of incremental change. It's the decision framework that breaks "big" into manageable "smalls," centering our focus on what's proximate and relevant. A marathon may be the end goal, but runners must finish the first mile before the next. There's nothing wrong with starting with the end in mind, so long as we're not leaping ahead, becoming overwhelmed, and then failing to start. From the beginning, marginal unveils the most sensible path of least resistance, revealing low-hanging fruit before climbing higher. Marginal works and endures because it's doable, forgiving, and progressive.

Doable

Whether we realize it or not, we are all marginal analysts and practitioners. It's how we make it through the day. We instinctively think and do life on the margin because we're creatures of habit and safety. Imagine if the shower's hot or cold blast was the binary decision facing us every morning. Few would shower or get out of bed. But thankfully, we're able to marginally adjust the knob back and forth till we get it just right. It's the incremental tweak that gives us the "doable" courage to step in, day after day.

—

Those who witnessed my face plant came to the rescue, marginally. No one challenged me to "do or die" and immediately flip again. Rather, they helped restore my broken ego and shaken spirit by showing me small but key adjustments. It was a series of baby steps that encouraged me to start again. From changes in technique to words of encouragement to providing a spotter, tearing down obstacles into bite-sized pieces enabled the journey to last. When the going gets tough, marginal breaks tough into what's doable.

Forgiving

Marginal rewrites the decision script by offering forgiveness amidst failure. Because marginal navigates step by step, mistakes are afforded opportunities to take a step back, reflect, and redirect as needed. Unlike totality's crazy big leaps that can crush failure in an instant, with marginal there's margin for error. We see this in financial investing. Dollar cost averaging invests incrementally over regular intervals, and diversification spreads the wealth across a wide range of assets. Both are weary of placing all their eggs in one basket. The former avoids the basket of lump-sum timing, and the latter avoids the basket of a single asset. Each method provides a hedge of protection against total loss. At the margin, success may be incremental, but so also is failure. It may not present the fastest route to the highest of highs, but it definitely mitigates the fastest route to the lowest of lows, and despite the worst of failures, marginal lives to tell about it.

—

In gymnastics, fear was the ever-present element, but forgiveness persistently overcame fear. There was no shame in crawling before walking. That was the norm. And when I was ready to run, I found forgiveness in the safety of spotters, harnesses, and padded mats. My teammates and coaches voiced encouragement at every turn, knowing that at the heart of improvement was the willingness to fail. Marginal's forgiveness allowed me to embrace failure as a source from which to learn and grow, not from which to sheepishly run and hide.

Progressive

Big aspirations have flashes, even seasons of inspiration, but they quickly lose steam when there's nothing more than willpower to sustain their possibility. To persevere, we need a sense of progress. That's why marginal doesn't hesitate to pursue even the smallest of wins— anything to create forward movement and momentum. Once progress has been tasted, the desire is for more. Progress begets progress, builds confidence, and inspires hope. It squashes doubts and strengthens courage. Progress also gains buy-in, offsetting skepticism and cynicism, and affording naysayers time to adjust and adapt. Successive progress is what sets the stage for major breakthroughs and giant leaps. We can glean from setbacks, but it's a lot more fun to learn from progress, no matter how small.

—

Later that season I finally learned to do a backflip, among many other gymnastics skills, but not through an all-or-nothing bravado. Each layer of difficulty was progressively overcome, step by step, spot after spot, fear over fear. And with time, a foundation built on trust, confidence, and courage was laid, turning steps into jumps and jumps into leaps. Perhaps it was too late for Olympic fame, but four years after the demise of my baseball dreams, I reached the Illinois state finals with a college scholarship in hand. The only high school tweak that may have proved larger? Inch by inch, I graduated a foot taller.

IS MARGINAL BIG ENOUGH? ONLY IF IT'S IMPORTANT ENOUGH

> It is nothing new or original to say that golf is played one stroke at a time. But it took me many years to realize it.
>
> —Bobby Jones

As someone who enjoys golf and its rich traditions, Bobby Jones stands as one of the most influential figures in the game's history. Founder of Augusta National, home to the Masters, Mr. Jones once confessed that the marginal nature of golf, though plainly evident, took a long time to figure out. How could someone deeply familiar with the game find it so difficult to appropriate that which was obvious? To believe and trust that marginal is enough, we have to embrace what seems counterintuitive and countercultural.

Counterintuitive

When goals are lofty and the vision is grand, we stare at marginal and think, *That's it?* What significant dent can incremental possibly make? The bigger the stakes, the more we think we need to go big and do more. It's how we're wired—"big needs big" to overcome. Marginal seems too small to be the golden strategy. It's not big enough, fast enough, or the immediate difference-maker we need to meet the magnitude of the moment. We seek a decision framework that fits our mountain-sized situation and can soothe our impatience.

It's not that marginal doesn't appreciate the occasional home-run swing, knockout punch, and hole in one, but it knows that a solid dose of singles, jabs, and putts are often far more consistent and impactful. It seems counterintuitive that less leads to more. To accomplish big, we need to stay the course with small. To succeed swiftly, we should proceed steadily. And to leap, we must persistently crawl. Over the course of a lengthy tournament, many crescendos and climactic moments will come into play, yet every stroke carries an equivalent weight on the scorecard, from the first to the last. To race ahead or linger behind does disservice to the swing at hand. The game hasn't changed, but it's our psyche that's at play. Embracing "one at a time," no matter the situation, was a simple but profound lesson for Mr. Jones and for us.

Countercultural

For all its doable, forgiving, and progressive attributes, marginal can be painstakingly redundant and boring. It lacks that fast-paced, instant gratification that appeals to a consumer culture. We're captivated by how-to videos far more than by books that reveal purpose. In a generation of unprecedented speed, information, and social influence, where riches, relationships, and fitness appear a click away, the path of marginal comes across as both unnecessary and old-fashioned. Who has the time, patience, and maturity for such a cautious approach? The notions of grinding it out, enduring ups and downs, rebuilding a foundation, and chipping away at challenges all begin to sound laborious. Take investing, for example. Does anyone in our crypto and day-trade world follow the principles of diversification and long-term growth anymore? And so we abandon the crawl of marginal, and often prefer the dangerous leaps associated with extremes. It's countercultural, then, to seek solid footing at the margin, but doing so isn't a concession by any means.

—

To commit to a journey at the margin is to embrace both the counterintuitive and the countercultural. It's only when our perspective of "big" is seen through the lens of "must achieve and must last" that we give marginal the proper attention it deserves. We suddenly appreciate being patient enough, detailed enough, slow enough, redundant enough, and even boring enough in how we move forward. We no longer look for shortcuts, but instead ensure that no steps are missed—because it's about building the strongest foundation possible, one that can face our mountain-sized situation and still last. One-hit wonders and fly-by-night trends need not apply. The more important, transformative, and enduring the endeavor, the more marginal makes total sense. Sometimes the degree of a step's importance may not be evident till further down the road, and that's OK. Marginal has a way of unfolding importance as well, step by step. Marginal doesn't cater to those in a hurry or those with fleeting goals. It caters to those who are committed to seeing something amazing that will last. When it comes to big importance, small was always intended to be the most effective, consistent approach.

OPENING SHOCK! SETTING THE STAGE FOR A TOTAL LEAP

I feel listless, with cold, clammy hands. Stomach churning, mouth salivating. Just utter the word. But the noise is deafening. As I stare down into the abyss, the wind rages with unbridled fury. Words elude me. Suddenly there's a sharp slap and piercing command that cuts through the storm. I react. I leap. What have I done?

At the United States Air Force Academy, I was presented a choice between two aerial programs: soaring gliders and free-fall parachuting. I chose free-fall, the Academy's "most intense character-building" program. Led by an elite cadre, the training was touted as best in the nation. From dawn till dusk, each day was densely packed—what to do, what not to do, how to jump, how to fall, and how to land. And of course a checklist for every contingency under the sun. We recited countless procedures and simulated their corresponding movements, synchronizing words with body positions. Redundancy's goal was twofold: mental and muscle memory. Every aspect of the training was methodical and meticulous, but the greatest emphasis was placed on the fundamental count: Slap thousand, Two thousand, Three thousand, Four thousand, Five thousand, Six thousand, Seven thousand, ARCH thousand, LOOK thousand, PULL thousand, CHECK thousand. When falling at a terminal velocity of 120 miles per hour, completely detached from the rest of the world, this count would be our guide and savior. Before the close of day one, we all knew the count and its move-ments by heart. The entire training might have lasted only a week, but the mundane repetition made it seem like an eternity. Cocky and im-patient, we swore we were ready days before. The last night of training, the tradition was to gather around and watch Faces of Death, *a video compilation of tragic outcomes. Of course, one of the clips was a sky-dive gone wrong. A bit spooked, I ran across the quad to my friend who had earned his wings the week prior. I asked for one word of advice, to which he chuckled and said, "You know that count? You'll forget it." Was he joking? I might forget the countless contingencies, but not the count. Not a chance. I lay in bed mumbling, "Slap thousand, Two thousand, Three thousand . . . ," before falling fast asleep.*

The alarm sounded, and an hour later we were off to the flight line. The time had finally come. Fully geared with chutes packed, fourteen of us boarded the first plane. I was number fourteen, sitting in the last seat. Once the required altitude was met, the plane would cycle in an oval formation, dropping one person at each end. For me, that meant a long, bumpy ride. Next to the exit door was our jumpmaster—our in-structor, demonstrator, coach, and now mother hen, ready to push her chicks out of the nest. As the plane climbed, our excitement surpassed it, and by the time we reached altitude, it was a full-on party. Above the noise, the jumpmaster shouted our last name followed by "Stand in the door!" The first cadet crawled to the exit as trained. Once in position, the jumpmaster gave one last thumbs-up, then slapped their backside and commanded, "Go!" Through fogged goggles, I saw him jump. And just like that, he was gone. The finality was surreal. Would I ever see my friend again? With each disappearance, the cabin became an emptied tomb. No amount of simulation, repetition, and words of advice could have fully prepared me for reality's extreme. By loop five, I was dealing with more pressing issues. Anxiety had accelerated my predisposition to airsickness. Only two more loops. Hold it together. I wanted to alert someone, anyone, but I couldn't speak without fear of ridicule—and upheaval. It was now the final loop . . . just me and my jumpmaster. "Paik! Stand in the door!" Training instinctively dragged me the length of the plane toward the exit. Lifeless, I knelt at the door—heart pounding, engine blaring, wind blasting. Against my better judgment, I looked down and saw all of Colorado Springs sectioned into miniature squares, matchbox cars lining I-25. The count was still alive and swirling within me, but it had abruptly changed to "Back out now" thousand, "About to vomit" thousand, "I'm going to die" thousand, "Don't do it" thousand. Just as I was about to speak, there came the force of the slap and the shout, "Go!" And without a word, I jumped.

MARGINAL—WAS IT ENOUGH?

Literally and figuratively, that was the most terrifying, undesirable leap I've ever taken in life. It was bigger than big and went against every rational bone in my body. Why didn't I speak up, and how did I leap when every part of me said no? Look no further than the marginal steps that preceded it. Despite the many complaints under my breath, the program and its cadre knew exactly what they were doing. I'm sure I wasn't the first to consider retreating at that final moment. There was a method to their marginal madness, and it proved itself from start to finish. Meticulous, repetitive, redundant . . . memorization, recitation, simulation . . . questions, feedback, accountability. Over and over again. The training didn't have to be long in duration, but it needed to be definitive enough that no one would depart from it while under duress. When done right, marginal doesn't just move objects at rest, it pushes doubts, fears, and resistance straight out the door.

—

Falling, flopping, tumbling. All went blank. Fear had made me retreat into the fetal position and all I could see flashing before me was blue, green, blue, green . . . the accelerated exchange between sky and ground, heaven and earth. I was somersaulting downward at record speed, thinking, I'm going to die! *Would I be the first fatality in the program's history? My friend was right, I had completely forgotten the count.*

TOTAL PARALYSIS IS REAL

Just because we've built a foundation at the margin doesn't mean it always carries over. I thought forgetting the count was impossible, but total paralysis can kill marginal analysis instantly. Also known as decision or choice paralysis, it happens when there's sensory or information overload causing someone to freeze, unable to react. Circumstances and thresholds may vary by individual, but the shock waves create a common response: to retreat, hide, and shut down. I was at its brink before the leap, and definitely after. Overwhelmed by an environment and sensation that was beyond foreign, I shut down and retreated into the fetal position. It was too much to process all at once. Sadly, this happens often in relationships where one partner overwhelms the other by dumping "total feedback" on them. I recall that in the early years of marriage I would do what my wife called "vomit feedback." I tended to suppress what could have been handled gently, until suddenly feedback's cumulative effect would unexpectedly be unloaded in its totality. Not only would it crush my wife's spirit, but it would cause her to retreat and shut down, sometimes for days. I thought I was being open, honest, and constructive. And I should get it off my chest, right? Wrong. Total feedback totally hurt her, and trying to undo the damage on the spot was futile. Sadly, I've done the same with my kids, and whenever I have, the results have been the same—total shutdown. Whether in quantity or severity, total feedback is too much for anyone to absorb all at once.

The problem with "total" anything, whether it's drastic feedback or drastic change, is that the mind, body, and soul aren't given the time or space to process. It takes an extraordinarily high level of resilience for anyone to immediately receive, adjust, and adapt. Total paralysis is a showstopper. For us to get the best response, we need to walk people from where they are to where they could be, marginally.

—

Pulling the rip cord while tumbling was on the list of top three mistakes, but what choice did I have? I was diving toward death. Miraculously, at the height of panic, mental and muscle memory kicked in. But in fact, it wasn't a miracle—it was marginal. All the training, repetition, and redundancy is what kicked in. The foundation painstakingly built on the margin held together . . . damaged, but strong enough to snap me out of total paralysis. Most of the count may have disappeared, but one word was all I needed: "ARCH." We had repeatedly been told that if tumbling should occur, ARCH. I shouted, "I don't want to die!" and found myself repeating, "Arch, arch, ARCH!" and my body instinctively followed suit. Instantly I went from a tumbling fetus to a stable leaf. It worked! I then immediately cried, "Look, look, LOOK!" And locating my rip cord, I finally yelled, "Pull, pull, PULL!" The chute flared open. The gravitational pullback, known as opening shock, yanked my body, causing me to unleash the most violent projectile vomit. Every bit of pent-up anxiety and fear spewed across Colorado Springs . . . and it was the best relief ever.

A FOUNDATION BUILT TO SURVIVE—A TRUSTWORTHY PROCESS

There's a reason the program was touted as the best. To guarantee our survival under extreme duress, there could be no shortcuts to this trustworthy process. As with the backflip, I thought I was ready to free fall on day one. But thank god no one trusted me. Rather, the foundation was built to trust the marginal process. When "do or die" literally means do or die, and everyone has a unique response to stress, trust cannot be placed on anyone's individual ability or confidence to make the leap and survive. The marginal process was intended to serve the lowest common denominator, and every detail was designed to battle that person's worst enemy in free fall: themselves. Isn't this the case in most of life's uncertain and chaotic adventures? Don't we find ourselves to be our own worst enemies? The program understood that students would overestimate their ability to overcome the challenge while underestimating the intensity of that first fall. That's why the cadre were sticklers about redundancy and excessive in their drills. We may have been grumbling about the duration of the program, but it was about absorption rate. Every minute of the seven days was necessary to provide adequate time and repetition for the training to sink in. Our survival depended on a foundation built on depth and quality, not speed. And consequently, the cadre never fell prey to our grumblings or anyone's desire for instant gratification. This was the way of marginal—building the right fundamentals and forming lasting habits so we would execute and not fully crack under pressure. That we were able to face the fog and friction of total paralysis and still survive was a testament to this strong, trustworthy process.

—

The marginal foundation held firm. Mental and muscle memory led me toward an instinctive solution despite that worst enemy swirling in my head. It overcame total panic and total paralysis, and ultimately it was able to overcome me. As my limp body slowly fell to the earth, I was grateful to be alive. But never again. Once was enough. I had no interest in doing it four more times to earn my wings. I was convinced I had violated every major safety requirement and was certain to get kicked out, which was fine by me. I approached the watchtower, where several instructors, including my jumpmaster, had gathered. Every free fall was closely monitored and evaluated through a telescopic lens. The director pulled me aside. "Paik, that was quite the exit." He then asked, "Any idea how long you were falling?" What felt like an eternity ended up being six seconds. I was awaiting my disqualification when my jumpmaster approached, gave me a pat on the back, and said, "Nice recovery. Next time, don't go back into Mommy's womb. And don't forget to count." What did he mean, "next time?" I wasn't kicked out? Everyone had a good laugh regarding my projectile vomit and the next thing I knew, I was back on the plane. But this time, in the first seat.

A FOUNDATION BUILT TO THRIVE—THE ROLE OF MARGINAL CATALYSTS

While I was expecting to get the boot with total feedback, I instead encountered the opposite—forgiveness, incremental advice, and words of progress. We can either be a marginal catalyst or a total showstopper. That day I had leaders who were marginal catalysts who understood that most journeys are, first and foremost, a "character-building" program. Yes, there are situations where development will need to take a back seat to immediate performance and results, but more often than not such dire emergencies are the exception. If the military can take a developmental approach with eighteen-year-olds free-falling out of planes, then I think we can all take a similar approach to most of life's experiences.

Emphasis is placed on the journey more than the destination. Any successful coach will say the same: "Focus on the journey and the destination will take care of itself." This gives catalysts freedom to use both positives and negatives as means for correction and growth. Marginal catalysts hold the right perspective about journey over destination, character over performance, and today because of tomorrow.

Marginal Catalysts Emphasize Marginal Feedback

Constructive feedback is best served marginally. Focusing on a few key things, or one main thing, helps to pinpoint where we most want others to focus. After all, not everything can or should be "most" important. A simple way to communicate emphasis is to just say it: "If you only remember one thing from this lesson, remember ARCH." And then say it again and again. Streamlined focus is critical to moving forward with the right thing(s) rather than half-heartedly or confusedly toward everything. Ask, "What's the top priority today? What's the one change, the one improvement, the one goal we want to accomplish?" The distinction can be as plain as "What's on our plates?" versus "What's the *top* thing on our plate?" Then follow up by asking, "How did that one thing go?" Singular emphasis helps prevent total paralysis and encourages immediate action. Dumping versus delegating, as shown in chapter 3, is another example. Dumping is a form of total overload, and it can be overwhelming without marginal guidance and direction. Delegating prioritizes, narrows, and eliminates distractions and unnecessary tasks, so we can help others focus forward. I could have easily been dumped on after that first jump. There were so many things I forgot and did wrong. But the catalysts kept it simple and in good humor: great recovery, don't go back into Mommy's womb, and remember your count. And they didn't need to remind me to sit in the first seat.

Marginal Catalysts Break Things Down

The less theoretical the better, especially when we're discussing urgent matters. Goals and tasks need to be broken down in ways that can be immediately pursued and knowingly accomplished. If that's not possible, then it may not be as urgent as we think. As for broader concepts such as core values, company culture, vision, strategy, and mission, marginal catalysts don't assume general comprehension or wide adherence. Instead, they attempt to break these down to where everyone can understand and discuss them in relevant terms. If for some reason we're unable to do this, then perhaps we don't quite understand the concept's building blocks ourselves, and revisions should be made.

How many vision and mission statements have we heard where interpretations vary or the language is so lofty and vague that it makes no practical difference? When the big picture gets lost or confused, details that follow will undoubtedly suffer. Marginal catalysts view and communicate the big picture through the lens of daily relevance. When they do this consistently, it will change how people think, believe, prioritize, and behave at the margin. Our training was the best and safest in the nation not because of grand visions and the number of students churned, but because we had marginal catalysts committed to breaking down challenges into the execution of countless small steps that everyone could understand and follow.

Marginal Catalysts Plan to Forgive

Marginal catalysts expect failure, not perfection. They realize that mistakes are a regular part of any journey but that forgiveness is easier said than done. Therefore, the best catalysts have the foresight to anticipate accordingly and create "margin" for error. They invoke contingency planning and add buffers where possible. One basic method is to schedule deadlines well in advance so as to mitigate the pressures of last-minute surprises. To avoid all-or-nothing, do-or-die scenarios, catalysts establish milestones and perform regular checkups to stay on track. Some might view this as micromanagement, but it's more in line with "trust but verify." Marginal catalysts also add in flexibility by building financial reserves and maintaining backup personnel. No catalyst wants their hand to be forced by a resource crunch. The more adaptive their plan, the greater the margin for error and the freedom to forgive.

Marginal Catalysts "Push Out" for Growth

It's one thing to nudge forward, it's another to push outward. Marginal catalysts know how and when to push others. When people are trained, have formed the right habits, and have journeyed in character, it's time to get them out the door. Sending others toward new challenges and heightened responsibilities is the outflow of progress and the exposure needed for continued growth. Catalysts must network, research, and line up opportunities for this very purpose. One of the greatest ways to reward and inspire others is to invest in their educational and professional development. The willingness to push out, even to our own immediate detriment, is the ultimate vote of confidence to catalyze growth in others.

—

As terrifying as that first jump was, it paved the way to the next. I had just survived, but the cadre were confident it was time to thrive. My failure was forgiven, and adjustments would be made. It became all about the next step. For me, knowing what not to do was as significant as knowing what to do.

Sitting in the front seat, I felt far more at ease as we climbed in elevation. The time had quickly come for my second jump. "Paik . . . stand in the door." I thought, No matter what happens, I'm not going back into the womb. With a firm slap and the word "Go!" I leaped—but this time, a perfect exit. "Slap thousand, Two thousand, Three thousand . . ." I counted aloud while floating away. Without tumbling, I saw blue skies all around. "Four thousand, five thousand . . ." I could see my jumpmaster in the doorway, smiling and waving at me. I waved back. "Six thousand, Seven thousand . . ." No longer paralyzed by fear, I felt an inexpressible joy and exhilaration. "ARCH thousand, LOOK thousand, PULL thousand." The chute opened on cue. It was the unimaginable, the unfathomable, the impossible, and I never wanted it to end.

After completing five jumps, I graduated and earned my wings. From near death to hoping it would never end, from arrogant start to humble finish, it was a journey sustained at the margin. How does anyone work up the nerve to leap from a perfectly safe plane at fourteen thousand feet? To jump solo, completely detached from the world? To move from fear to dare, again and again? The power of the tweak.

DELIVERING HOPE

For my last Air Force assignment, I had the privilege of serving in Germany. Exploring Europe as a family was a dream come true. While speeding along the autobahn, I would often wonder, Where would all this be if not for the Berlin Airlift? *One of the major crises during the Cold War period was the Soviet blockade of allied-controlled West Berlin. The blockade prevented the flow of outside resources to a war-torn city, cutting off life-sustaining support to more than two million Berliners. It was an act to force the United States and its allies to relinquish their control. But doing so would potentially open the door to the rest of Germany and Western Europe. Sometimes it's good to pause and consider what direction world history would have taken if, at that pivotal moment, the Soviets had succeeded.*

The US and its allies responded by airlifting resources into West Berlin from bases in Western Germany. It was an aerial resupply chain unlike any other, with planes landing every minute of every day for nearly a year. Operation Vittles, as it was appropriately named, delivered more than two million tons in critical supplies despite the assortment of planes and shoddy runways of 1948. It was this commitment to success that finally convinced the Soviets to relent. Overcoming the blockade is considered one of the greatest military achievements of the Cold War and in the history of airlift. I viewed it as a miracle.

As amazing as this was, there was a smaller operation, a marginal one embedded within, that may have proven more profound for Germany's future. It's the story of a young American pilot known as the Candy Bomber or, more affectionately, "Uncle Wiggly Wings." While walking the barbed-wire fence line, this young lieutenant encountered a group of German children and proceeded to hand them two sticks of gum. Instead of taking it for themselves, he noticed how the older children apportioned the sticks to as many as possible—and those who missed out sniffed the wrappers. At that moment, he decided he would regularly deliver candy to Berlin's children during his airdrops. He and a few friends pooled their rations and tied pieces of candy to parachutes made of handkerchiefs. He told the children to look for his plane by the way he would "wiggle" its wings. The practice continued until one day, word got out and made its way to the airlift commander. The pilot was sure he'd face discipline for his unauthorized actions. But instead, the commander announced that the candy drops would be officially sanctioned under the title Operation Little Vittles. The general saw its value in winning hearts and minds. News quickly spread, and soon donations from confectionary companies across the US poured in. By the time the Berlin Airlift concluded, more than 250,000 parachutes totaling twenty-three tons of candy had been dropped.

Years later this pilot returned to the same base, but now as its commander. He received a visit from a young woman who said, "You don't know me, but we all know you." And in her hand was a handkerchief. "You may have been dropping candy, but to us you were delivering hope." One piece of candy, one parachute, one act of kindness, one marginal drop of hope at a time—this was one "wiggly" catalyst and the power of his tweak. These were the thoughts that ran through my mind as I drove the autobahn and gazed upon Germany's beauty.

I had the great privilege of meeting Colonel Gail Halvorsen, the Candy Bomber, as he was promoting none other than a children's book to once again inspire future generations at the margin. He was as humble and compassionate in person as I had imagined. In 2022, he passed away at the age of 101, leaving behind a quiet legacy that in many ways, perhaps, changed the world.

BE A CATALYST FOR HOPE

Nothing inspires the human spirit more than hope. Even a single ounce can change the course of world history. Throughout my life and leadership, marginal analysis has always reminded me that a word or act of hope is often the most important tweak. More than learning a backflip, hope rescued me from shame. More than leaping from a plane, hope restored my character, courage, and confidence. And more than delivering candy, hope revived a war-torn generation. If there's one tweak that keeps the struggling and weary soul moving forward on their journey, this is it. If you're going to give advice and constructive feedback, narrow it down to one or two manageable points—but make sure one of them is hope. This is a gift with which leaders must seek to be generous. We don't need to change the world, just tweak it.

CONCLUSION

What fear or obstacles do we face? What small, doable steps can we take? Is there a touch of forgiveness and a drop of hope we can give today? Are we breaking down total into marginal or paralyzing others? I love witnessing life's milestones. Whether graduations, promotions, retirements, or other personal and professional accomplishments, there's usually a common thread—stories of character journeyed at the margin. No one gets to where they are overnight and without their share of ups and downs. That's what makes reaching the milestone so rewarding. Though it's a product of long-suffering, the triumphant finish confirms that the counterintuitive and countercultural were always the intended path for the greatest achievements. And standing alongside, we see a cloud of catalysts—a stream of coaches, teachers, spouses, siblings, parents, friends, and mentors who persistently nudged, pushed, pulled, yelled, and forgave at the margin. It takes a village. Leaders, this is our privileged calling and special platform—to catalyze the lives of those around us. We hold to the marginal process and its unbreakable foundation so we may repeatedly stand at the door and with confidence shout, "Go!"

CHAPTER 5

DIMINISHING RETURNS— LEADING REST

A day when one has not pushed oneself to the limit seems a damaged, damaging day, a sinful day. Not so! The most valuable thing one can do for the psyche, occasionally, is to let it rest, wander, live in the changing light of a room.
—May Sarton

BLUF: Fatigue, frustration, failure. Has the strain set in? Do you feel its resentment? How tragic to witness a journey of good intentions run out of steam, then fall apart. There's a fine line between building a foundation at the margin and destroying it by pushing beyond the point of no return. We may not always be able to persevere with focus and vitality, but it's quite another thing to endure to the point of exhaustion, with self-pity and complaints. If we strive to run with composure to the end, inspiring those who follow, then diminishing returns must be our steady beacon and guide.

—

Back when unleaded gas was eighty-nine cents and my trusted GPS was the Rand McNally Atlas, I set out on my first expedition across

America. I was twenty-five, en route to my third duty station. From Pennsylvania to California, the goal was thirty-four hundred miles in seven days. But by the time I reached Mount Rushmore, I had taken far too many excursions and was a day behind schedule. Montana had no speed limits and its highway was barren. This was the green flag I needed. My little Toyota reached speeds I never thought possible, and if I motored through the night I could make up significant ground. But as evening wore on, the mental fog rolled in. No matter how loud the stereo or how many mouthfuls of sunflower seeds, lengthy stretches turned into mindless blurs. Perhaps in a subconscious plea for an exit, I arbitrarily changed lanes, though no other cars were present. Just as I maneuvered, something in the distance reflected in my high beams. There was no time to react. It was coming from the eyes of a large silhouette. As I zoomed past, standing motionless to my left was a giant buck. Miraculously, I had switched to the "right" lane and missed death by mere inches. Heart pounding, I finally decided to pull over, slowed to a rest area, and within minutes fell fast asleep.

DIMINISHING RETURNS—THE UNIVERSAL DECLINE, UNIVERSALLY IGNORED

Diminishing returns is the nature of any persistent stand-alone activity. Good, bad, or indifferent, every singular activity eventually tapers toward fatigue. It doesn't matter who, what, when, where, or why. There are no exceptions or exclusions, and scarcity is the universal cause. Nevertheless, this principle remains universally ignored. If we're not suppressing it behind the late-night wheel, we dismiss it while pushing the limits at work or at the gym, during finals week, or while out partying with friends. We witness diminishing returns all around us yet rarely blink an eye.

I grew up with parents who worked seven days a week for more than thirty-five years. My wife runs her own business while juggling multiple activities and interests, just hoping no ball will drop. My boys keep exercising despite whining about muscle aches. My daughter collapses from her social schedule, forgetting she's a closet introvert. And

I swear my puppy, Lulu, has FOMO, ceaselessly playing, licking, and barking till she drops flat on the floor. It doesn't end there. Across my community, I see a pastor in his twenty-sixth year of ministry who's never taken a full sabbatical; an ENT surgeon who continues to operate while suffering from back pain; a neighborhood mom shuffling between boardroom and family room, from corporate sales to four kids and two dogs; a general counsel whose golf round consists of more calls and texts than total strokes; and perhaps topping the list, our dear friend who is physically blind yet her social, travel, speaking, volunteering, and parenting schedules leave all of us in the dust. Love you guys . . . but how does a community extend calming advice when we're all constantly speeding?

DIMINISHING RETURNS—THE NONUNIVERSAL RATE

Diminishing returns may be our most hypocritical principle. Most honest résumés should include the title Chief of Diminishing Returns. However, let me qualify this by saying that not all bouts of diminishing returns are signs of detrimental behavior. The principle may be universal, but we each have our unique saturation points and tolerance for pain. What goes up must come down, but where we peak and how we spiral remains a subjective mystery. This is what makes diminishing returns both complex and dangerous. Consider alcohol consumption. As drinks flow, happy becomes happier, but where happiest occurs and what happens thereafter depends on the individual. For some, the happiest buzz may come with a single drink (my wife); for others, it may take several rounds before we feel the slightest effect (me). The rate of ascent, the point of plateau, the rate of descent, and the consequences thereafter all vary by person. There's no quantitative standard by which to decide "when to say when." It takes *qualitative* insight . . . a level of self-awareness and discipline. After graduating SERE (survival) training, a bunch of us drove to an all-you-can-eat pizza buffet. I was salivating from the start and set out to consume everything in sight. While several members of the group made us proud, I was stuffed after two slices. But who eats two slices at a pizza buffet? Ignoring the signs of diminishing returns, I went well past them. At first the decline seemed slow, but then it dropped vertically, and the evening's joyous event came to a crashing halt over the toilet. Slow and gradual for some turned out to be swift and severe for me. We experience diminishing returns subjectively. Hence, it requires that we go deeper to prudently assess ourselves and others.

WELCOME TO THE PUZZLE PALACE

I had all but forgotten my occupational specialty. After three years of teaching, the Air Force decided it was time for me to jump back into financial management (FM) but at the highest level: the Pentagon. My first day at the puzzle palace coincided with the new rank of major, but it wasn't a cause for celebration. The promotion carried with it heightened perceptions of expertise and leadership in one's field. To make matters worse, I was assigned to the infamous Engine Room, arguably the most demanding FM role among peers. To bear its grueling 24/7 commitment was a badge of honor, but of all the jobs to slowly acclimate to, this was not it. As I was lost and in a hurry, my wife performed the unceremonious pin-on in the parking lot before I rushed off.

I was warmly greeted by my desk mate who held the same rank but was leap years ahead of me in corporate knowledge and experience. I confessed how ill-prepared I felt and apologized in advance about being his new partner. But with complete reassurance he said, "Seung, I got you. Don't worry, I'm the pilot and you're my copilot." What a relief. The learning curve was steep, but I wouldn't let him down. Our responsibility was resource integration. This meant reviewing thousands of pieces of data, including every weapon, person, and dollar comprising the Air Force budget for the next five years. The database to build the enormous master file was an antiquated, 1960s flat-file system developed during the Kennedy administration. The graphics consisted of a blinking white cursor on a black screen. No mouse, no cut and paste, and no edit/ undo. Every step was manual, sequential, and completely unforgiving. My colleague and I were the sole gatekeepers. Nothing entered or exited the database without our engagement, and what we declared as "locked" stood as the Air Force's official position to the rest of the world. The work was high volume and labor intensive, but it had to be accurate, complete, and on time. Our credibility before Congress depended on it.

DIMINISHING RETURNS BEARS EXTERNAL AND INTERNAL PRESSURES

The degree to which we push the limits on diminishing returns is often the result of both pressures. External pressures are those outside our control, a fact of life. Being assigned a reputable office in the Pentagon, responsible for Air Force credibility, and piloting a complex system for congressional deadlines felt like a mountain of external pressures. Internal pressures, on the other hand, were derived from self-expectations and personal anxieties. I carried a chip on my shoulder from the start, needing to prove my worth and wanting to live up to the new rank as quickly as possible. My lack of both proficiency and experience in this pressure-filled environment was a recipe for disaster. Grand illusions mixed with internal and external pressures kept me stoically pressing forward when I should have been raising the red flag early and often.

—

The lead was a different breed. I rarely saw my colleague eat, but he never appeared hungry. Not once did he go to the gym, but he was the most fit of all the people in the office. And despite the long hours, there was no intake of caffeine or sunflower seeds on his part. He was consistently pleasant, professional, and helpful, bending over backward for others. There were countless errors he could have returned, but he always took it upon himself to make the revisions, staying late into the night so others could head home. No matter the stress level, I never saw him lose his cool. I once wondered, Is he the lone exception to scarcity? *In the end, I couldn't have asked for a better partner and lead pilot, but as next in line, it was miserable knowing I'd have to fill his shoes.*

Don't Compare, Be Self-Aware

With the right perspective, comparisons can fuel a healthy competitive spirit and serve as motivation to stretch limits and establish new thresholds—but only with the recognition that going from zero to hero typically follows a marginal journey. By trying to *keep up* rather than *develop up*, we lose patience in striving after the best version of ourselves and, instead, sprint toward an unmatchable version of someone else. To refrain from such comparisons, we need a steady dose of self-awareness. This means acknowledging our limits, being OK with saying no, and initiating proactive steps to recharge. It means having the courage to slow down and regularly find rest. I know, easier said than done.

But we've already established that the term *universal* does not imply a standard saturation point or a standard rate of decline, and definitely not a standard response to that decline. Whether the difference is due to genetics, training, and/or experience, whatever the reason, *we must constantly remind ourselves that no two people have identical capacities for anything.* We each plateau, spiral, and tap out at different times and in different ways. Therefore, it's senseless for us to compare and try to keep up. There was no way I was ever going to match my partner's proficiency in the time allotted; I should have been pacing myself toward the best version of me. But with that chip on my shoulder, immersed in a "no pain, no gain" culture, I kept pushing myself, trying to keep pace in hours, productivity, and demeanor. I continued to suppress my built-in warning system.

—

My time finally came to take the coveted lead. We were less than three months from submitting the annual President's Budget. With the lead stepping back, I would be the one to pilot it home. As expected, it was an all-out sprint to the finish. Weeks turned to days and days into hours. My bloodshot eyes could barely see, yet I raced ahead, loud stereo and sunflower seeds replaced by coffee and adrenaline. There was no time to pull over. The pressures were mounting, but this was all too important.

As my partner offered assistance, I pridefully reciprocated with the nod he first gave me: "Don't worry, I got you."

With only days till database lock, I kept driving through the night in a mental fog. A couple more keystrokes and a few more uploads, then I'll pull over. But suddenly my screen went blank and the cursor stood frozen. I should have switched lanes. I tapped several keys, but no change. I double-checked everything—keyboard, monitor, every cord and cable. All intact. I pulled out the extensive troubleshoot manual, but where to begin? I remained confident as my partner now jumped in. In our year together, there had never been a problem he couldn't solve. That is, until now. Several hours passed before we finally conceded. The system's administrator could only suggest that we power down and reboot, which would mean losing everything since the last update. My partner then asked, "Seung, when's the last time you backed up the master file?" At this late stage, it should have been hourly, but with no speed limits, I had been cruising along for days without backing up the data. For the first time I sensed panic as he voiced the Engine Room's familiar words. "Call your wife . . . it's going to be a long night." I had single-handedly wiped out the entire United States Air Force data file. Five years' worth of information and eleven months of updates gone. If only I had pulled over sooner.

Don't Be Fooled by Total Quantity and Momentary Boosts

I love the episode in *Seinfeld* where Jerry flies first-class and is amazed by the amenities—over-the-top service, softer pillows, gourmet food and drinks, and of course homemade chocolate chip cookies. While he's lavished in extravagance, the flight attendant asks, "More of anything?" To which he responds, "More of everything!" And in first class, who can blame him? There's more quantity and quality to be had. We all want to have our cake and eat it too. But when it comes to diminishing returns, an either/or trade-off is what's at hand. Keeping all else equal, we can attain either more quantity or more quality, but not both. We just have a hard time accepting that. I wanted to sightsee liberally across America and still make it on time to my next duty station. I wanted to prove I could complete the Air Force database just as well as, if not better and faster than, others before. *More of anything? More of everything!* But with diminishing returns, something's gotta give. And more often than not, it's the invisible that loses out to the visible, and the unseen that gives way to the seen. I like to think of myself as a person of quality, but when I'm under the gun of timelines and metrics, quality quickly takes a back seat to quantity's more tangible and measurable features. As long as I was gaining total distance on the road or completing more files in the database, the manner in which I did it was an afterthought. If shortcuts to quality meant more quantity, I took it. Both alertness and compliance declined, but I couldn't and wouldn't see the quality cliff in front of me. My focus was on quantity and its continued increase.

With the aid of temporary injections, what I call momentary boosts, quantity can muscle through for a time, but not quality. Boosts like added grit, spikes of adrenaline, and even material substances like caffeine, loud music, and sunflower seeds can temporarily advance quantity, but quality demands more. It requires a level of clarity and concentration that temporary boosts cannot sustain. Imagine an exhausted surgeon continuing to operate on momentary boosts. Or a commercial pilot, overscheduled and overworked, surviving on catnaps and caffeine. I'd hate to be their patient or passenger. In any profession where quality is of the utmost importance, consumers should be able to trust that the service providers are well rested. But sadly, that's not the case when total quantity is the prevailing metric. Quality and compliance didn't matter enough for me to stop, and they weren't transparent enough for others to intercede. Instead, tangible gains running on the fumes of momentary boosts kept me pushing for more. Until we recognize the misleading nature of momentary boosts and total quantity, we will keep squeezing for more and expect others to do the same. *Show me someone who is focused on quality over quantity, and I'll show you someone who heeds the warning of diminishing returns.* More of anything? More quality, please.

We Don't See Because We Don't Want to Look

There are plenty of diminishing signs that are plainly obvious but intentionally overlooked. Before burnout there's stress, before anger there's frustration, before injury there's soreness, before collapse there's exhaustion, and before exhaustion, fatigue. Yet the more someone's activity has a direct bearing on the bottom line, the more likely we are to ignore the signs. Too often as leaders, we're willing to overlook their pain for our gain. Consider the following distress signals:

- change in physical appearance—disheveled, weight loss/gain
- change in attitude or demeanor—irritable, angry, argumentative
- persistent exhaustion—sleepy, lethargic, unmotivated
- little to no time for relationships—family, friends, community
- seeking escape—drugs, excessive entertainment/hobbies, shopping
- dropping basic responsibilities—unpaid bills, unkempt home and car
- forgetfulness—significant dates/events, redundancy, late/absent
- social disinterest—ghosting, disengagement, lack of communication

Rarely do these indicators appear suddenly and independently; they appear gradually and collectively. It takes a level of effort to notice their early onset, but it also takes a level of willful ignorance to later brush them aside. How often have we seen family members pushing themselves to the brink, yet because it's to our benefit, we don't say a word or intervene to assist? Just stop and think about who does most of the chores at work or home. Is doing that work truly to their comparative advantage, or are we simply not wanting to acknowledge their diminishing returns for our sake? If it's happening with loved ones at home, how much more are we turning a blind eye at work, in our organizations, and around our community when it's to our benefit. I sometimes wonder if remote work, despite all its advantages, will exacerbate this willful ignorance among leaders and managers, as our employees are further out of sight and out of mind.

One indicator might be subtle, but it's perhaps the most damaging:

the change in attitude. It's the unappreciated parent checking out amid stress and fatigue. It's the burned-out counselor struggling to find compassion and empathy. It's the overwhelmed ER physician forgetting bedside manner. A lengthy or permanent drop in attitude affects everything within and around, often leaving a trail of pain. It's the sad realization of having poured yourself into worthy investments, only to arrive at a place of brokenness and regret, having jeopardized the very ideals and relationships that you most valued. Former CEO of Coca-Cola, Brian Dyson, describes it well: "Imagine life as a game in which you are juggling five balls in the air. You name them—work, family, health, friends and spirit—and you're keeping all of these in the air. You will soon understand that work is a rubber ball. If you drop it, it will bounce back. But the other four balls—family, health, friends and spirit—are made of glass. If you drop one of these, they will be irrevocably scuffed, marked, nicked, damaged or even shattered. They will never be the same. You must understand that and strive for balance in your life." If we can be aware of the ubiquity of diminishing returns, we can lead from the front and transparently address it together. But we have to be ready and willing to look and see.

—

With only forty-eight hours remaining, it was impossible to recover what was lost. I was still the lead but no longer a hero. In humility and scarcity, I returned to econ's tried and true. I buried what was lost, especially my ego (sunk-cost fallacy); started with the easiest files, the low-hanging fruit (opportunity cost); gathered the help of others (comparative advantage); and step by step, recreated the largest programs dating back to the last update (marginal analysis). In the end we ran out of time, and not every detail made it back into the Air Force program. We took all that was left undone and lumped it under a generic title, Balancer, a self-made margin for error. It was a painful conclusion to submit an end product nowhere near the Engine Room's standard of excellence, but on this occasion, getting it done had to be good enough. The database was officially locked.

DIMINISHING RETURNS: EXERCISING GRIT AND RESILIENCE

Just because we experience diminishing returns doesn't mean we should automatically begin retreating. Sometimes we need to dig in and run further into the fire. There are seasons and surges where we may need to "embrace the suck" for a time. It may be required to meet the significant purpose at hand or to get to where we want to be. It's common when starting a new job or launching a new career, when we become parents or go on deployments. There are professions where pushing beyond fatigue is the vocational norm—that's true of athletes, surgeons, nurses, rescue workers, investment bankers, entrepreneurs, commercial truckers, restaurant owners/chefs, and being in FM at the Pentagon. Temporary spikes are also expected for tax accountants, students during finals, or volunteers during a humanitarian crisis. And sometimes it's a rite of passage, as with medical school, boot camp, or a business start-up.

When It's Worth It—Alignment to Expectations

The question of "when to say when" then doesn't center solely on diminishing returns but must also focus on both grit and resilience: What's our capacity to endure diminishing returns—to both withstand it and to recover quickly from its negative effects? Just as diminishing returns is subjective, so also is an individual's grittiness and resiliency. They're muscles that need to be exercised and strengthened in order to steadily rise to the occasion. But as with any type of strength conditioning, it must start with proper alignment to achieve its intended purpose. Is the worth and the duration of an endeavor in line with our expectations? This is a crucial consideration in emotionally and psychologically absorbing diminishing returns. The right frame of reference can greatly alter our subjective capacity, jump-starting the necessary grit and resilience to make it safely through. We may not be able to overcome diminishing returns altogether, but having the right alignment can go a long way in helping us grin and bear it.

The list of notable endeavors above isn't meant to be exhaustive. Rather, it's to remind us that going above and beyond the point of diminishing returns should carry an expected worth and duration that's definitive. When it comes to grit and resilience, to be forewarned is to be forearmed. Diminishing returns doesn't bode well under the elements of ignorance and surprise. *No one knew it was going to be this hard. What did we get ourselves into? Who moved the goalpost?* When our capacity gets shaken by doubts, ignorance, or questions of duration, we're likely to lose our psychological and emotional edge. Leaders who are mindful of this will make a concerted effort to eliminate such things in the lives of their people and will do so by providing as much clarity, consistency, and certainty in their communication as possible. Grittiness and resiliency depend on it.

When It's Not Worth It

If worth regularly fails to materialize and surges rarely seem to fade, then "temporary" may be more permanent than realized. When "this too shall pass" has no end in sight, it can desperately exacerbate diminishing returns. Far more than productivity and performance, one's quality of life and overall health may dangerously be at stake. We must find this to be intolerable. Even in pursuit of the worthiest of endeavors, people need to take a break and sense that some level of relief is on the way. To continue irregardless is not just negligent but may prove downright derelict. Should tragedy occur, the world should rightfully demand, "Could they, or someone, have known better? And if so, what should have been done?" If going beyond the point of diminishing returns results in long-term or irreparable damage, then the prior concerns of productivity or performance will have hardly mattered. When people are left defeated and/or removed from the fight, then even from a productivity standpoint, that's the worst outcome of all. The Great Resignation during the recent pandemic placed a spotlight on this very concern. Workers bucked the long-lasting traditions and societal pressures that kept driving us forward, teetering on the insatiable edge. Those traditions weren't worth it, but somehow we allowed them to become the accepted norm. Wellness is the greater priority we should all hope to reclaim, and it begins by reexamining our own values.

Apart from this, we may continually find ourselves in an untenable yet often self-inflicted position.

—

The sad part about that late night in the Engine Room was that I didn't need to continue behind that wheel. I grossly overestimated the value of persisting and tragically underestimated the likelihood and cost of one fatigue-driven mistake. I realized immediately, but too late, that pushing through wasn't worth it. No one was going to die and the Air Force wasn't about to shut down because of anything I did. Before the master file was deleted, we were actually in a good place, at a good stopping point. Voltaire said it well: "The best is the enemy of good." If there was one positive about our crazy culture, it's that no one even wondered why we were working around the clock. And since no one knew how to do our jobs, no one knew in real time if we were doing it right or wrong. We kept my "accident" private as there was nothing more we could do and no point in alarming everyone up the chain. It wasn't until months later, when we received an inquiry about several programs missing their budget, that we coordinated one-on-one with the necessary program offices and restored their missing details from the "balancer." Everything else went under the radar. It was a crash for the ages, but if a tree falls in the forest and no one hears it, does it make a sound?

LEADING "SUBSTITUTIONARY" REST

A year later, with unforgettable lessons in hand, I was now able to "lead" by prescribing rest for myself and for the new copilot who would become my successor. Vigilance for diminishing returns was imperative and led to proactive engagement. This meant taking initiative, being intentional, and regularly communicating. If signs of burnout are observed, engage immediately, not later. I invoked the concepts of self-care and buddy-care, knowing our culture in the Pentagon wouldn't. I realized such care isn't selfish—in the long run, it's truly selfless and mission enhancing. I knew from experience that no one was going to give us rest, so it became something we had to carve out for ourselves—scheduled time off, lunch breaks, and the push to make it home in time for dinner even with the DC commute. We held each other accountable to this as much as we held each other accountable for work. I was reminded that no two people spiral downhill the same way, at the same rate, with the same results. So it was important to ask subjective questions, qualitative questions, and sometimes personal questions—to check up on his well-being and to make sure his home life was going OK. And our personal conversations led to a much closer friendship. We also incorporated fitness into our work schedule, purchasing Pentagon gym memberships. We weren't always successful at getting in our workouts, but we were far better than the year before. Finally, I learned and passed along assurance that, together, there wasn't any mistake from which we couldn't recover. Therefore, rest didn't need to be a last resort, but the chosen priority toward excellence.

From a process standpoint, the biggest change we made involved comparative advantage. Ours was to perform the final checks and uploads, not to make everyone's corrections. Rather than being the single fixer of all errors, the new process was to return files needing correction back to the submitters, with deadlines. This wasn't favorably received at first, as people had been enabled for so long. And many times it felt inefficient, as it would have been much faster and easier to fix the errors ourselves. But in the long run it broadened our base of experts. And over time, the number of corrections became significantly less, saving us countless hours and stress, especially during crunch time. It drastically alleviated our technical burdens and enhanced our ability to focus on our comparative advantage. We may have been the gatekeeper of the database, but many hands were needed to fulfill their individual roles.

SUBSTITUTE REST WITH REPLENISHMENT

Let's face it, we live and work in a society where grit and perseverance trump balance and harmony any day of the week. Pushing oneself to the brink is not only expected, but praised and rewarded. Such a culture will rarely prioritize less over more, quality over quantity, rest over stress. This same tone extends into the home. We all have loved ones who ask for more than they give and never think twice. And children, gotta love 'em, but they can suck us dry. With friends and family, as well as at work, if wellness is compromised to the point of *detrimental* returns, then even the most noble pursuits risk losing key soldiers in the battle. Wouldn't it be better to just heed diminishing returns and choose rest before it chooses us? Either we pursue it, or it will find us in unfortunate ways. We need people who are not only willing to take rest, but to lead rest for others. Otherwise, many won't do it.

As poet May Sarton, in *Journal of a Solitude*, so accurately assessed, a day of rest seems a "damaged" and "sinful" day. So how do we lead rest without feeling guilty or getting marginalized? And what does "rest" from diminishing returns really mean? First, it doesn't mean escaping from priorities and responsibilities. Avoidance and procrastination only add stress and fatigue down the road. It also doesn't mean sitting around all day eating bonbons. Opportunity costs and marginal catalysts will eventually have something to say about that. Perhaps a better, more descriptive word than rest is *replenishment*. After all, I still had a cross-country drive to finish, and I still had a deadline due to Congress. Continuing with renewed vigor means refilling our empty tanks. Hence, replenishment isn't just about idly pulling over. It's about plugging in and getting supercharged.

True rest from diminishing returns is substitutionary rest. And to be a leader of this strategy means both exemplifying it and setting a tone others may follow. As with diminishing returns, there's subjectivity in what may or may not replenish each individual. Therefore, the following discussion isn't intended to be comprehensive or prescriptive, but to get our juices flowing so we may brainstorm ways that are the most personally effective.

SUBSTITUTE MOMENTARY BOOSTS WITH LASTING ONES

Unlike momentary boosts that help us muscle through before a sudden drop-off, lasting boosts aim to reinvigorate the mind, body, and soul with the goal of endurance. They build resilience for today and for the journey ahead.

Boosts for the Diminishing Mind

Resting the mind doesn't mean vegging out. It means making a mental switch and giving the fatigued mind a change in scenery. It's switching our thoughts from that which is fatiguing us to something that might renew and inspire us. Basketball Hall of Fame legend Phil Jackson—winner of eleven championships as a head coach, the most in NBA history—hand-picked books for his players, ranging across a variety of topics, but always with intent. As a former professional player, he understood the pressures and the mental grind of a long season, and that the last thing his players needed was *more* basketball. He viewed the mind as a complex muscle that shrivels with monotony but flourishes when stretched, exercised, and diversely challenged. Decades later, former players still talk about the books he gave them.

Another boost comes from clearing the mind of clutter, taking time to organize, prioritize, and eliminate things in our lives. Perhaps it's hard to have a restful mind because we've been procrastinating with (blank) and now things are piling up. Decluttering the mind means doing the things necessary to add space and clarity for peace of mind. If that means finishing off those bills, do it. Or if decluttering the mind is aided by decluttering your house or car, do it. And it definitely means managing your screen time and trying to unplug a bit more. One change my kids made was substituting their haphazard approach to studying with the pomodoro technique. It parceled study sessions into timed spurts with timed breaks in-between. Sounds simple, but it includes the rule that you must eliminate all distractions during the study blocks—no phone, food, etc. Those are only allowed during the timed breaks. Nothing fancy, but incredibly effective. It decluttered my kids' study habits and catalyzed activity, efficiency, and consistency, while defeating procrastination. It not only improved duration (quantity) but also heightened concentration and retention (quality).

Note: Technology—legit or false boost? It may be useful by aiding in efficiency, organization, and expediency. But it also carries a 24/7 burden. Technology is never off, creating an around-the-clock culture with its expectations. Without fixed, physical boundaries, we're always within reach. It takes an extra measure of discipline and pushback for technology to be the boost it could be. Or it may be the most dangerous false boost of all.

Boosts for the Diminishing Body

We could all use a bit more sleep. But regular, undistracted sleep takes work. It means getting to bed on time, putting away late-night distractions, and refraining from foods and substances that may disturb sleep. In other words, a level of discipline precedes rest for the diminishing body. Whether altering your sleep schedule, improving your diet, or undertaking a new fitness regimen, bodily rest seeks a lifestyle change—active for inactive. For exercise, it's about picking a program that works for you and sticking with it. It might mean signing up for that gym membership or joining that spin class and Pilates group to add accountability and consistency. During the pandemic, our family incorporated HIIT workouts, High-Intensity Interval Training. They're exhausting, but effective and efficient, perfectly suiting our minimalist approach. We also prioritized recovery with cold showers and ice, proper hydration, and plenty of stretching. Last but not least, protein shakes and massage-gun sessions became a daily practice. We may have been under the strain of house arrest, but we kept our bodies active and replenished, which made a huge difference in our attitudes at home.

Boosts for the Diminishing Soul

Finding rest for the soul means remembering that we're more than just the sum of our parts, that our identity and significance stand independent of worldly metrics, and that we have purpose and meaning far beyond the numbers. As our minds and bodies need continuous nourishment, so also do our hearts. We need food for the soul to savor all that is priceless—hope, love, peace, joy, and contentment. Replenishing the soul is an acquired practice that extends into all areas of life. It's learning to be still and introspective, perhaps through prayer, meditation, or certain breathing techniques. It's recentering our outlook and connecting at a deeper level to our thoughts and emotions. It might involve getting away for a quiet retreat or finding a place of solitude to journal. It might mean putting on those headphones and listening to music, creating and appreciating art, or simply being still in nature. It's about substituting the busyness of life for moments of contemplation and reflection. Sometimes that inner peace is found in support groups, counseling, and therapy. And often it's found in a community of faith through fellowship and worship.

For the two years my family lived in Japan, our lives intersected with those of seven other military families on our block. Our connective bond was faith, and every Friday evening, after another exhausting week, we would break bread together, take time to study the Bible, share burdens, and pray for one another. By growing in fellowship and doing life together, our group became a "resting place" for everyone's heart, mind, and soul.

SUBSTITUTE YOUR ROLE WITH REPLACEMENTS

Happiness is having backups. The best feeling is when we can rest in the excellence of teammates, ready to take the baton and run even faster (recall chapter 3 and comparative advantage). Consider baseball's relief pitcher. Rarely does a starter in any sport maintain the same vigor from start to finish. Yet in their competitive spirit, many will argue to stay in the game. Driving at max capacity may periodically succeed, but it also potentially empties the tank for peak performance when it matters most. The best coaches understand this and are unwavering about substituting with fresh replacements, not only for the sake of the team but for the sake of every player during a long season. Intuitively and statistically, they manage through pacing, keeping bench players active and engaged while conserving starters for the long haul. When teams can build a replenishing force of replacements, no individual loss becomes a single point of failure. This provides rest and reassurance for everyone, especially those in positions of leadership.

When I deployed to Afghanistan, we hand-selected an experienced, highly reputable reservist to come and fill my shoes in Germany for seven months. After a week of intensive overlap, she took my seat and never looked back. It was such a relief to be able to deploy and not worry about a thing regarding my team and the mission at home station. It gave me freedom to completely focus on the mission down-range. No one should be indispensable if diminishing returns are inevitable. And we all should aim to train and mentor our way out of a job, at least temporarily, so we can deploy, go on sabbatical, or take a vacation without any mental reservation.

SUBSTITUTE QUANTITATIVE WITH QUALITATIVE ASSESSMENTS

We know we're taking diminishing returns seriously when we're willing to consider quality over quantity. Instead of emphasizing autogenerated numbers and quantitative metrics, try seeking after individual and subjective feedback. For starters, build a tiger team and begin the discussion. Ask members, "What are diminishers that cause burnout, increase anxiety, and hurt effort and motivation? What are some telltale signs of fatigue in the organization? Do we ask about morale, attitudes, and motivation as much as we do about productivity and performance?" They're not necessarily correlated. Qualitative research doesn't require a huge sample size, but it does require a thoughtful list of introspective, impactful questions. And it requires dedicated time to absorb and assess the information. We need to get comfortable with feelings, opinions, and personal experiences as a measure for assessment. Methods for gathering information may include conducting sessions on lessons learned, climate surveys, customer feedback, product reviews, focus groups, and in-depth interviews. If greatness is our pursuit and detrimental returns is the danger, then we absolutely need to establish and assess qualitative metrics as much as we do quantitative ones.

SUBSTITUTE SLOGANS FOR A CULTURE WITHOUT STIGMA

Elon Musk said, "There are way easier places to work, but nobody ever changed the world on forty hours a week." Instead of disagreeing with

Mr. Musk, I'll just add that nobody ever changed the world on zero hours of rest either. Is rest properly understood and esteemed in your workplace, or is it generally the last resort? I'd ask, "Are we building a championship culture or an organizational hell?" Holistic wellness leads to championships, and the best leaders understand that rest and hard work are not mutually exclusive. In fact, it's because we esteem hard work and relentless effort that we also esteem the need for substitutionary rest. If what we consistently exude is "no pain, no gain" and "what doesn't kill us only makes us stronger," then vigilance toward self-care and buddy-care won't have a chance. What doesn't kill us can still put us in the hospital, and that doesn't help anyone. And so we must continuously expose and battle the stigma—that rest is for the weak, the lazy, the undedicated souls destined for failure, but not for the strong, the die-hard, and the gritty. We must be in this together; it's not a competition. We can all succeed and finish on top. But vigilance about rest must be modeled by the leader. Vigilance doesn't turn a blind eye but is pursuant and accountable. It assumes the worst and therefore asks hard questions, is intentionally observant, and is ready to engage.

Leaders, our calling is to set the tone for both work and rest, both quantity of production and quality of life, both excellence and "good enough." Instead of squeezing more out of everything, our message should be "To squeeze best, get some rest." For tomorrow, we squeeze again.

SUBSTITUTE OPTIONAL FOR MANDATORY REST

Sometimes a culture is so geared toward mission and sacrifice, with long hours and the subsequent burnout, that it might make good policy to mandate and enforce rest. Leadernomics practices holistic wellness because it best serves life, health, and safety and produces the greatest potential for overall job satisfaction, productivity, performance, and longevity. On Thanksgiving during my assignment in Japan, our neighborhood decided to do a progressive dinner, hopping from house to house. But one of our fighter pilot neighbors had to bow out on short notice due to "crew rest," his compulsory twelve hours of undisturbed time prior to flight duty. I tried knocking on his door several times to persuade him to join us, but he came to the door only to say he wished he could. The rest was mandated and held sacred. And it made perfect sense. No one wanted a fatigued pilot flying a multimillion-dollar jet, possibly with munitions. But as I walked away, I remembered thinking, *Why wasn't there any mandatory crew rest when I was "piloting" the database?* Those in the business of protecting life, health, and safety are vigilant about making rest a part of their professional culture. It's encouraged, expected, required, even regulated. And rightfully so. If only we imparted a little more of this to every busy, stressed-out station in life. Over the years, each military service has studied fatigue analysis across a wider range of career fields, not just operators, to assess the effects of diminishing returns in all our service members. To our military's credit, they've been asking the hard questions, being proactive and accountable to others. As a result, they have created metrics and mandates for rest at critical junctures to ensure peak performance. But ultimately it takes a leadership that understands the subjective nature of diminishing returns, and has the courage to invoke the appropriate, vigilant care before it's too late.

CONCLUSION

Who could use the gift of rest?

—

My fondest farewell memory is from our community in Japan. Busy with the mission, my wife and I found ourselves scrambling to the bitter end. An overseas relocation meant an endless checklist, everything from selling vehicles to gathering school transcripts and medical records. Between household goods, donations, personal baggage, and storage, we were just thankful not to have packed one of the Paik kids. After two full days with movers, the house was a disaster and we were well beyond the point of diminishing returns. But our final inspection was scheduled for the next morning, and the house needed to be spick-and-span to pass.

That's when we heard a knock on the door. It was our vigilant neighbors, crashing our home with buckets and rags and bleach in hand. Before I could say a word, they asked, "Where do we start?" And all through the night, this husband and wife team cleaned alongside us. What had been a stress-filled, miserable week that culminated with another mountain . . . turned into an unforgettable farewell, energized and revitalized by friendship, laughter, and the sacrifice of service. With renewed vigor, we tackled this last responsibility together. Where there was no time for a break, we found rest in their shared assistance and presence. Leaders understand the universal and subjective nature of diminishing returns and the power of substitutionary rest. Rest is the gift we must vigilantly seek to give and encourage. Responsibilities don't end, but leaders know to knock on the door and arrive with no stigma . . . just some bleach.

CHAPTER 6

INTERNALIZING THE EXTERNALITY— LEADING CULTURE

Culture eats strategy for breakfast.

—Peter Drucker

BLUF: Culture is a force to be reckoned with. It influences individuals and shapes social norms. It drives organizational behavior and dictates company direction. But it's also sensitive and responsive. Culture isn't determined by chance or meant to preserve the status quo. Rather, it's influenced by the same body of people that it influences. In other words, culture is collectively decided by us—what is or isn't expected, what is or isn't accepted, and what is or isn't internalized. If we take command of culture, culture will take care of our command.

—

November 12, 2016. It was a calm, quiet morning in Afghanistan. The predawn 5K run would jump-start a slate of activities commemorating Veterans Day. I felt particularly proud to celebrate this occasion while deployed in a place where nearly one million Americans had come to serve. As I set out for the event, I realized it was much darker and colder than I had anticipated. So I headed back to my dorm to gather more gear. Shortly after I began backtracking, a loud explosion reverberated beneath me. The detonation occurred within eyeshot of where I'd been standing just minutes before. It was a suicide bomber. He killed five Americans and wounded seventeen others. A year later, the official investigation revealed that the attack had been months in the making. The bomber was a former Taliban insurgent who had been cleared to work inside the wire. Detailed findings indicated that standard procedures for hiring controls, background checks, daily escort duties, and disciplinary actions had all fallen by the wayside. The report tragically concluded that the attack was an outcome of "a pervasive culture of complacency." That's a familiar warning in the military profession. We know it as the enemy that's always lurking, on and off duty, ready to devour. Complacency kills. Yet "pervasive" conveyed something far more egregious. It meant that complacency had spread like cancer, permeating across attitudes and behaviors. In what was still an austere and hostile environment, how could we have so easily dropped our guard? The assessment was damning. A culture that should have sounded the alarms had allowed complacency to become the norm.

EXTERNALITIES: THE GOOD, THE BAD, AND THE UGLY

Externalities are spillover effects experienced in society. Some are good and defined as positive externalities. These contribute a measure of social welfare. Benefits that extend from a public garden, a beautification project, the pleasant aroma from a local bakery, or the sweet sounds of an open-air concert are all examples of positive externalities. Conversely, negative externalities extend the opposite. They produce a level of social harm. When a factory emits pollutants, the corresponding health hazards present a spillover cost onto society. Regardless of the company's awareness or intent, society is left holding the bag. Where it gets ugly is when negative externalities are left unchecked and uninhibited. We can appeal to conscience and to their sense of duty, but without proper incentives or any measure of consequence, self-interest is bound to fail society's best interest.

—

By 2016, the mission and makeup of America's military footprint in Afghanistan had changed drastically. The mission had shifted from combative to noncombative and from leading to supporting. Our role now was to teach, train, and advise. And with this shift, the majority of personnel flipped from military to civilian. The media even relabeled the conflict a "contractor's war." Upon arrival there, I found myself surrounded by contractors, government civilians, third-party foreign nationals, and local Afghans. While my team was fully armed from head to toe, we'd be standing next to multitudes wearing nothing more than khakis and collared shirts. The environment was eerily casual, and the contrast between the military minority and civilian majority was palpable. Furthermore, under the auspices of NATO training and advising, we had enjoyed a lengthy period of "security and success" from the rear. Command authority may have remained with the military, but the culture was decidedly not militaristic.

The list of findings from the bombing investigation showed that, spillover after spillover, vigilance slowly lost its grip. Over time, negative externalities had been allowed to run amok, and social norms followed suit. The "contract culture" ate vigilance for breakfast, and it was only a matter of time before tragedy struck. To point at a scapegoat on the ground would have been myopic at best. The fact of the matter was, culture had made an about-face toward complacency years earlier as the drawdown and change in mission produced an assortment of externalities that were never addressed or internalized.

INTERNALIZING THE EXTERNALITY

There's little cause for anyone to alter unfettered behavior without three key factors: expectations, incentives, and accountability. First, expectations: There must be standards by which people are assessed and evaluated. Whether broad or specific, they need to be clearly communicated rather than assumed. Second, incentives: These must be aligned to expectations so as not to contradict one another (i.e., perverse incentives). Incentives (including disincentives) are meant to guide behavior toward the direction of expectations. Third, accountability: This means exacting a price where the price is due by following through with the incentives. It's one thing to create incentives, it's another to consistently carry them out and see them through. To internalize the externality, we need all three: clear expectations, proper incentives, and consistent accountability. But we also need credible leadership, leaders who are committed to following up and following through. This is our model for establishing the right culture, a culture that promotes the good and doesn't turn a blind eye to the ugly.

NIGHT AND DAY—A LESSON FROM THE CLASSROOM

While teaching at the Air Force Academy, I decided to undertake an extra challenge to improve my pedagogical skills—teaching night classes at a nearby civilian college. The difference in student demographics and classroom behavior was night and day. I was impressed by my older students. Many were married with children, carrying full-time jobs. Yet they were on time and ready to engage. Their good attitude, presence, preparation, and participation were all positive externalities in the classroom, contributing toward everyone's engagement and learning. On the flip side, I had more than a handful of younger students who regularly came late, were ill-prepared, and would doze off at some point in class. Whether it was their general disruption, lack of participation, snoring, or bobbing heads, they were an unavoidable distraction, a negative externality. I never sensed any ill intent, but their obvious disinterest and body language detracted from the learning environment. Therein lay a clash of externalities. If both positive and negative spillovers were left unchecked, which classroom culture would prevail? I wasn't about to wait and see.

This was new territory for me. At the Academy, the institutional

culture and the social norms surrounding academics were well estab-
lished. Students generally policed themselves and each other, and if
they didn't, a simple word from the instructor was all it took to alter
their behavior. That wasn't the case here. My expectations for class-
room conduct were clear, but alone they weren't enough. I could tell
my good students were getting annoyed, and so was I. To promote the
desired behavior, I needed to intervene with the right incentives and ac-
countability. Both had to be consistent and credible for change to occur.

In terms of incentives, I would "tax" those who were causing social
harm and "subsidize" those who were contributing social good. Taxes
included a verbal "wake-up," one-on-one feedback, a penalty on grades,
and, if the behavior persisted, a note to administrators requesting the
student be dropped from my class. Each progressive tax was intended
to drive home internalization, making the responsible party bear a cost
for the spillover inflicted on others. In holding them accountable, there
would be no free lunch with negative externalities, and thankfully, I
never needed to levy that final tax.

To those who were prepared and actively participated, producing
a positive spillover, the incentives included public praise, extra credit
on assignments, and letters of recommendation for those who consis-
tently contributed toward classroom excellence. These were rewards to
recognize and further subsidize their positive behavior. As the semester
unfolded, the class as a whole moved in the direction of expectations,
incentives, and accountability. Not only did the sleepers follow suit,
but the overall culture began to change. What I didn't expect was how
quickly the change took a life of its own. No longer was I the driving
factor, but the students themselves were policing and encouraging each
other to pay attention and participate. I no longer needed to regularly
intervene. This was the power of social norms to produce the desired so-
cial outcome. I may have been the authoritative figurehead setting the
tone, but it was now culture that was clearly in command.

WE WANT CULTURE TO LEAD CULTURE

Imagine if the source of the negative spillover and harm is also the
spoon that feeds you—i.e., your employer or a factory that provides

your community with jobs. Or consider spillovers that get lost in a crowd: secondhand smoke, noise pollution, a rubberneckers' delay, or the all-too-common free rider. When external spillovers are painful to confront, hard to identify, and/or too vague to assign given the anonymity of shared duties and transient spaces, how do we exact a price where the price is due? And then, as I witnessed in Afghanistan, when complexities have permeated so deep and persisted for so long that externalities are defined as culturally pervasive, how and where do we begin? What's the remedy? And most important, how do we sustain a renewed culture for the long haul?

Simple. It just takes 24/7 hands-on, eyes-on monitoring with perfect information and perfect insight. It takes perfect wisdom and discernment to determine the exact incentives and disincentives to hold all behaviors perfectly accountable. And it takes (in)credible leaders who are consistently engaged, communicative, committed, and courageous. In other words, forget about it. Trying to address each and every externality with perfect outcomes is impossible, and it was never meant for any single individual to attempt. Instead, we must go back to marginal analysis and allow small to be our *big* guide.

The classroom example may seem far too simple and straightforward for more complex and advanced scenarios, but marginal analysis would beg to differ. By publicly and consistently addressing externalities through expectations, incentives, and accountability, I saw the classroom culture begin to change. With it, new social norms began to appear and gradually take over. More than any particular person or leader, it was the changed culture itself that increasingly became the primary influence over individual behavior. Call it a good "peer pressure," if you will. Getting to this place requires commitment and consistency, but this is what we as leaders want because no one can do a faster, more precise job of identifying and addressing externalities than those who are most proximately affected. They just need to know that internalization is a leadership priority, and that everyone is empowered to act. My good students had enough, and once they knew my mandate was credible, it became open season. The good students were now incentivized to police the bad actors and they did so in a caring manner—nudging their neighbors safely away from the tax and toward the greater good.

Internalizing externalities may not always affect culture as fast as it did in my classroom, but it does eventually happen. Culture is merely a composition of the people who comprise it. As they go, so goes culture and vice versa. Therefore, internalizing externalities must ultimately be about inspiring, empowering, and relying on everyone to do their part. Patient and committed leadership is the key in positively affecting the desired culture. This is where the strength and clarity of foundational concepts like vision, values, purpose, and mission absolutely matter. They represent the cornerstone from which culture's foundation is being built, and they unite us in something bigger than our self-interested behavior. When we can inspire internalization from a solid foundation, it lends depth to the expectations, incentives, and accountability set forth. This is where culture is ready to go next level—people not only doing their part, but willingly and proactively challenging others to do the same. Leaders may come and go, but when we can ignite this type of ping-pong effect across an organization, a culture has a sustainable chance at transformation. We see this in championship cultures, in organizations and on teams, where culture is *the* priority. It rules over individual preferences, seniority, rank, reputation, and positions. Anyone is permitted to challenge anyone who's not in line with the culture. Individuals need to get on board or the culture will run them over.

But the opposite is also true. When a solid foundation is absent or the cornerstone gets changed or compromised—when standards no longer have that connective strength to core values, vision, and purpose, something bigger than ourselves—a culture of toxicity may equally develop and persist. Negative peer pressure and bullying in schools, cutthroat competition at universities, public shaming and manipulation on social media platforms, fear and intimidation in the work center, pervasive complacency as the accepted norm . . . these are a few examples.

Positive or negative, good or bad, the cornerstone from which we build and how it informs what we allow and accept in the way of expectations, incentives, and accountability ultimately determines the culture ahead. So I ask: What's the desired culture that you envision? What's the strength and clarity of the cornerstone from which it's being built? And what will you allow and accept in the present culture?

Leaders, our job isn't to change culture overnight or to define its path from beginning to end. In fact, most of us won't be around long enough to see its full blossom. Instead, we're to be a catalyst and a consistent source of influence wherever we're planted so that the desired culture may have a chance. It's about setting the right tone and beginning the hard work of internalization. There's no sugarcoating the level of attention and effort required. But when we can answer the questions above and commit to the required steps, get ready to witness a new culture begin to take shape . . . and perhaps, even take command.

NEEDS OF THE AIR FORCE— TRANSFORMING A BROKEN CULTURE

The more senior I was in rank, the more the "needs of the Air Force" transitioned from slogan to my reality. It meant dropping my agenda and expectations for whatever the Air Force deemed imperative, regardless of any promises that were made to me. Such was the case with our abrupt diversion to Okinawa, Japan. Kadena was the largest Air Force base in the Pacific, and I was about to inherit an organization ranked dead last in every financial metric. Because of our size, we singlehandedly pulled down the entire region, placing it near the bottom of the Air Force. We were rolling the dice with defaults, delinquencies, fraud, and the destruction of government property. There were concerns about criminal behavior, including some of our base leaders. It was a sad state of affairs, and as the primary steward of funds, our organization was miserably failing the American taxpayer.

It was past midnight when we landed. My family fell fast asleep as I lay restless. At the break of dawn, I decided to sneak a visit to my new office incognito. I didn't expect to see a line of airmen outside, stretching from the front door to the back of the building. Inside, more were encamped across the lobby floor. I squeezed in next to a young airman trying to take a nap. He was nineteen and new to the Air Force, but already making his third visit to the office that week. Direct deposits had not been processed and his personal checks were bouncing. He'd come there straight off the night shift; my organization was the last place he wanted to be. I cringed at his initial impression of life in the Air Force. As I stood up to leave, the young airman sighed, "This place sucks." And as its new commander, I couldn't have agreed more. The "needs of the Air Force" were loud and clear.

START AT THE TOP: CULTURE'S LOW-HANGING FRUIT

The externalities of a broken culture rarely reside with one person, but there's no better place to start than at the top. My predecessor was someone I had known and respected for years, one of the nicest guys you could ever meet—knowledgeable, generous, and compassionate. His work ethic and dedication were beyond reproach. But the relentless pace at Kadena eventually took a toll. He became buried in an avalanche of responsibilities and decisions from which he couldn't surface. One might say he was placed in an untenable situation, and I wouldn't disagree. But the manner in which he lost the struggle is what stood out. His office became a black hole, a hoarder's scene. Along every wall and behind his desk, folders and documents were piled high. Deadlines vanished into thin air as good intentions fell prey to decision paralysis. Instead of being the mover and shaker of government funds, our organization became their primary bottleneck. Members weren't getting paid accurately or on time, organizational requirements weren't getting replenished, and mission priorities were awaiting dollars. When the flow of resources hit a standstill, the base commander had seen enough.

Are Leaders Themselves the Primary Externality?

The implications of a diminishing culture may be subtle, perhaps masked by the dedication of a few. But our breakdown was plain to see. The process of transforming organizational culture must begin by examining leadership and their decisions (or lack thereof). This goes back to chapters 1 and 2 (sunk cost and opportunity cost). For the sake of a desired but forgone culture (opportunity cost), are we willing to examine our present leaders (perhaps sunk cost)? Leaders, are you willing to look within and assess your influence on culture, and more objectively, are you willing to be assessed by others? The past things, the broken things, the sunken things that need to get buried—are leaders burying them or are they allowing the negatives to persist, slowly burying the organization? Leadership externalities that detract from culture are often obvious but left unattended . . . because they're the leader. Forms of intimidation, bullying, passive aggressiveness, manipulation, fixation, favoritism, moodiness, decision paralysis, incompetency . . . the list goes on. Toxic and/or failed leadership, at all levels, is culture's low-hanging fruit that must be addressed. A culture has no chance at transformation apart from this initial leadership assessment. Are we ready to accept and perform this evaluation for ourselves and others? Cultural transformation, similar to individual transformation, must begin with some burying, starting at the top. And sometimes that means a leader's removal.

—

Internal solutions to our organization's problems had been presented but sat dormant. I challenged my leadership staff to explain why no one had moved forward with them, with or without my predecessor's approval. The most junior officer spoke up. "Sir, the recommendations are severe and will impact the entire base. We know we have lines out the door, but for now we're asking to shut off phones, reduce customer service hours by half, and mandate appointments instead of allowing walk-ins." The plan was draconian and counterintuitive. The young officer continued. "To be honest, sir, we don't answer phones anyway." It wasn't meant as sarcasm, but as an honest and desperate plea for help. For months, the team had been bearing externalities that were not theirs to bear. Most of the errors and fixes they were dealing with weren't due to their actions. But they were stuck with the costly responsibility. Without any reprieve, their performance and morale had spiraled beyond the point of diminishing returns. The team was running on fumes—mind, body, and soul. There was no time for training, let alone self-care. As the backlog of errors mounted, it became a race between quantity versus quality, and both lost. I asked the young lieutenant, "If these recommendations are approved, how long before we see improvements?" "Six months, sir."

Are the Right People Bearing the Price?

Instead of disappointment and frustration, the overwhelming attitude, both internally and across the base, was apathy. Far worse than low expectations are no expectations. Members resigned themselves to our poor performance, and the habit was to point the finger rather than accept any personal responsibility. No financial process was completed in a vacuum, yet everyone across the base seemed to have forgotten that fiscal compliance was a team sport. We each had our respective roles to uphold. Nevertheless, as the focal point for resources, my organization remained the fall guy. We bore the blame and suffered the shame for errors and delays that weren't ours to internalize. The price was excessive and being exacted from the wrong place.

For starters, we needed to ask more of our base members (customers). We could only do so much with forms and documents that were inaccurate, incomplete, and/or late. Customers weren't being held accountable, yet their failures directly contributed to our metrics. Taking corrective actions became a "tax" on my team rather than on the responsible party. This needed to change. Requiring customers to fill out a pre-visit checklist to improve completeness and accuracy was a step in the right direction. It was now upon their shoulders to submit the information correctly from the start. And if the checklist wasn't completed, we would reject the submission rather than waste more time tracking them down. This was exacting a price where the price was due.

Another major concern was my team's lack of self-care and training. Both had given way to nonstop distractions throughout the day. It was a price an inexperienced team could ill afford. We needed blocks of undistracted time to audit, train, and conduct self-care. Unplugging office phones, closing doors early, and moving to a system of appointments only was a price members across the base needed to absorb. We may have reduced our availability, but it was in order to get a better-trained, more energized team of financial experts. And in the long run, this would mean better performance and faster service. We couldn't conduct focused training while also being fully available to customers throughout the duty day. Growing in proficiency was too important to try and multitask.

Shifting internalization is never easy or popular. It often carries widespread negativity and false perceptions. Someone has to pay. It's just a matter of who and how much. Everyone demanded progress, but few across the base were willing to internalize their fair share to achieve it.

—

It came time for my first official meeting with the boss, the wing commander. After a few niceties, the conversation went as follows:

Me: Boss, I'd like to propose a few changes.

Commander: Approved.

Me: Sir, I think you'll want to hear what the changes are.

Commander: Approved.

Me: They're going to be disruptive and unpopular.

At this point, the commander cut me off once and for all: Seung, I've seen the metrics, and I've been to your building. Approved.

The message was clear: Enough talk, take action. He demanded leadership, and he demanded change. His only question was "How long until we see results?" I said six months. He countered with four. When I returned to my unit, I gathered the team. "The good news: The wing commander approved our recommendations. The bad news: We have three months to show results." A little fabrication never hurts to inspire urgency.

Has the Tone Been Set?

It was a brief but poignant conversation—any action is better than the status quo. Externalities required intervention, and the wing commander was ready to engage. He didn't need to have it all figured out to know that something had to be done. I never perceived him as a confrontational person, but he wasn't going to turn a blind eye either, or passively wait for change. He started by removing my predecessor, then continued by approving our draconian measures. Once I showed him Kadena's dead-last position, I didn't need to say more. The wing commander was a fighter pilot by trade and hated nothing more than losing, let alone being last. Standards, expectations, accountability, and transparency was how my boss approached internalization. His message to all subordinate commanders was simple and clear: Take ownership in fixing our fiscal culture or someone else will. In those few words, he was exacting a price where the price was due, and no leader was exempt.

BUILD SHARED PARTNERSHIPS—SIDE TO SIDE

The tone was set for me to conduct peer engagement. But initially this didn't go over so well. When I told fellow leaders our draconian course of action, the unanimous response was "Seung, are you out of your mind?" Limiting our availability meant longer lines and delays. And then, adding fuel to the fire, I told my peers that the commander requested by-name transparency at our weekly staff meetings. This would specifically highlight organizations and individuals, even fellow leaders, who were negatively contributing to our last-place metrics. Without advance warning and little explanation, fellow commanders perceived that I was throwing them under the bus. Peers were scrambling and frustrations mounted. I remember at social functions, my wife would ask, "How come no one is talking to us?" The public reveal of stats had a powerful trickle-down effect that quickly led to improved compliance, but it came at a cost. I learned an important lesson about building collegiality and trust.

Of all the accountability relationships, side to side may be the most impactful but also the most sensitive to navigate. No one sees each other's true colors more intimately than peers. Among fellow leaders, we know who is and is not carrying their weight. We know when peers are striving or coasting, mission-oriented or self-centered, and being honest or full of BS. But to gain buy-in and shared partnership, the relationship must always be centered around trust and respect. I may have had the boss's directive and full support regarding transparency, but in my zeal, I had failed to prioritize and establish this in our relationships.

What might have ended disastrously was rescued by the grace of two of my fellow commanders. They came to my office for assistance, but also reminded me that collegiality was a must. Anything less might

be perceived as cutthroat, undermining the very culture we were trying to build. This was sound advice. My peers needed to unequivocally
trust that I was out to support, not to attack. And I needed to express
externalities as "ours," not "mine" or "theirs." Collegiality meant approaching "our" externalities through patient assistance, giving more
than just fair warning. It required regularly communicating and coor-
dinating in advance so as not to openly embarrass or blindside anyone,
especially in front of the boss. This is how externalities were meant to
be internalized among peers—shared.

As we experienced progress, positive externalities began to show
forth. Instead of only presenting the "bad" list, I was now able to
highlight the good, publicly praising the success and improvements
made by my peers. This was a game changer in accelerating collegiality and trust, and in turn, fostered a greater willingness among
peers to internalize. This is what championship teams do when they
have players-only meetings. They may curse each other out for mistakes and failures, but it's to challenge, to motivate, and to lift each
other up behind closed doors, not for the world to see. It's the process
of policing one another with brutal honesty yet having each other's
backs.

*Note: While it's particularly important to go above and beyond in peer
assistance and support, we must be wary of "coddling" and "masking."
It's a natural development—the stronger helping the weaker, the expert
answering for the novice, the experienced covering the inexperienced.
And in the spirit of partnership, it's an easy line to cross. But it's an even
more difficult wall to jump back over. I gradually learned that many of
my peers had come to rely solely on my predecessor for all things financial. Whether it was a personal request or for their organization, they
got in the habit of going directly to him to correct, mask, or resolve. And
he always responded. Their inability to meet fiscal compliance became
enabled and caused externalities to persist. As the new guy, I came
in and cut off all "coddling" ties, but it was painful all around. Until
we made progress, it was not an easy stigma to overcome. For a short
while it may be collegial, but unless they're weaned off, the recipient
will never learn and do. Going above and beyond with peers isn't about
giving them a bone, but helping them to fend for themselves.*

BUILD COLLECTIVE OWNERSHIP—BOTTOM UP

From the top, then side to side, we now aim to build stakeholders from the bottom up. An externality is indifferent. It affects anyone and everyone standing in its path, regardless of position or rank. Yet the most widespread impact often befalls the most marginalized and unheard. They're at the bottom, where spillovers eventually settle. I would not have known the extent to which externalities were personally affecting airmen and their day-to-day mission had I not sat next to that nineteen-year-old my first morning. It's one thing to suspect from a safe distance; it's another to see the effects on others firsthand and to hear frustrations at ground level. Unless those "lowest" are given a voice, they will have no choice but to grin and bear that which is not theirs to bear, and leaders will continue to walk in ignorance or denial.

It's been a while since I've sat in a meeting where every voice was given an opportunity to be heard. I used to think this was the norm, but I've come to realize that soliciting inputs and constructive feedback is not a popular method for solving problems, especially in public forums where the rank and file may be present. Most meetings turn into a monologue rather than a discussion. Decisions get made unilaterally, and feedback is essentially uninvited. Sometimes the urgency of a situation may dictate this path, but this should be the exception rather than the norm when it comes to internalizing externalities.

No leader can pinpoint externalities from a bird's-eye view. Precise solutions require proximate engagement, and those closest to the ground usually have the clearest insight. If the desired culture is that everyone be part of the solution, then everyone should be welcome to challenge the status quo. Pursuing grassroots feedback isn't only a powerful means by which to achieve holistic buy-in, but it's often the most effective path to identifying externalities and exacting a price where the price is due.

—

We widely expanded our ears to feedback. If our organization was going to implement a disruptive course of action impacting those at ground level, they too needed to know they had a voice. We published Q and A articles in the base newspaper, committed to a twenty-four-hour turnaround on all e-mail inquiries, conducted town hall meetings, visited individual organizations upon request, and met regularly with various focus groups to hear their feedback and suggestions in person. We churned through customer surveys, categorized areas that needed specific attention, and publicly highlighted our progress along with best practices. Last but not least, we implemented "train the trainer" sessions to grow in-house experts in every customer unit. Through these forums, we carved a host of avenues for voices to be heard, inviting every person to become a stakeholder in our changing financial culture.

—

Setting the tone may come from the top, but a transformed culture isn't sustainable when it remains just there. The greater metric is in seeing internalization happen in every direction—side to side and from the bottom up. When we can reach across these levels, building partnerships and growing ownership, a broad change in social norms is made possible, and a renewed culture may finally breathe and take on a life of its own.

CHIEF: THE GODFATHER OF INTERNALIZATION

No one proved greater in altering our organization's internal climate than my senior enlisted advisor, "Chief R." He was the epitome of what chiefs in the United States Air Force were meant to be. I saw him as the Godfather of internalization, constantly making offers others couldn't refuse. There wasn't a person he encountered without asking, "How are we doing? Anything I can do to make things better?" He would take notes and never fail to follow up and follow through, building our credibility. His personal offer of service and self-accountability humbly disarmed any audience. He would then flip the conversation into a mutual request: "Here's where I could use your help." It was a simple exchange but conveyed a message of collective ownership and shared accountability. Internalizing the externality worked both ways. Each day for Chief was about taxing and subsidizing, exacting a price where the price was due and providing positive recognition and reinforcement where deserved. Though not an economist, he knew how to apply Leadernomics to internalize externalities and to transform a culture.

———

First, he stamped out futility and persistently focused on present attitudes and forward progress. While everyone had been weighed down by the negativity, Chief buried what was **sunk**, leaving behind our poor reputation and broken identity. This was a critical step toward a fresh start. Every morning began with face-to-face walkarounds, handshakes and greetings, and pats on the back. Most of all, he was a hugger. His direct eye contact and cheerful attitude left no room for a downcast soul. He displayed motivational signs and posters with inspiring messages, and once individuals stepped out of his revolving door, Chief was able to look beyond past failings and lay hold of the opportunities ahead. He didn't dwell on anyone's mistakes or our organization's past performance, but offered a clean slate for change.

Second, Chief valued **opportunity cost**. He esteemed the sacrifices of his airmen and was constantly building relationship bridges, finding ways to connect, and pulling airmen out of "Harm's Bay." Though mission minded, he was people first. On and off duty, he got to know their families, learned their preferences, and became aware of their concerns and aspirations. And no one hosted a better Thanksgiving meal and game of football than Chief. Slowly, he took a beaten-down, deflated corps of apathetic supervisors, and externality by externality appealed to their sense of duty and core values. Without compromise, Chief consistently gave tough feedback and challenged our midlevel supervisors with credible consequences. This reinvigorated the right social norms at the most critical level in our organization. He was hard on negative externalities, but no one praised the positive more than Chief. He enacted a robust recognition program, and most of all, made sure to give credit where credit was due. One by one, airmen were professionally transformed and their performances changed.

Third, Chief R relied on **comparative advantage,** seeking after everyone's contributory value. People just needed the right training and feedback, and then to be entrusted and empowered. He worked with supervisors to reassign duties facilitating specialization and exchange. There was one shy, insecure airman, who was junior in our organization, that Chief intentionally designated as our lead for morning runs. The initial going was awkward, but Chief had his back and everyone knew it. The airman wasn't the strongest, fastest, or most coordinated, but he had endurance and was able to run farther than most. With each session, you could see his confidence grow with his contributions. Not only did everyone's run time gradually improve, but with it, so did the airman's leadership development and overall duty performance. He may not have had an absolute advantage in anything, but he had a comparative advantage in this, and for the organization it was a win-win exchange. Chief searched for win-wins in everyone.

Fourth, with regard to **diminishing returns**, the team needed both a rod and staff. Chief was the first to hold our people accountable, but he was even bolder in defending their efforts and championing their needs. Any outside accusers would have to go through Chief. He protected their time and focus from the noise so they could eat, train, conduct quality control, and implement measures of self-care. Despite two shoddy knees from his youth, Chief exemplified the importance of fitness, participating in intramural football and basketball while building camaraderie with the guys. Chief wasn't swayed by platitudes like "No pain, no gain," or "Rest is for the weak." Instead he encouraged daily replenishment and buddy-care, calling on everyone to look out for each other. More than any quantitative metric, he focused on the qualitative measures surrounding his people, especially in challenging their attitudes. Surface behavior can quickly and forcefully be manipulated, but attitudes take time and space to evolve. Without a deep change in attitudes, no other change would last. Chief took a broken culture mired in fatigue and apathy and each day, slowly turned the ship around.

Fifth, talk about being a catalyst—giving feedback on the **margin** was Chief's hallmark. It was exactly what I needed to witness and learn for myself. When I arrived in Japan, I hit the ground running, giving everyone an earful of change from day one. The airmen generally appeared receptive because they had no other choice, but another group sat unphased—my Japanese local-nationals. Japanese citizens comprised nearly half of the base's civilian workforce, and their continuity was indispensable to our mission. The most senior civilian on my team had thirty-five years of service. I didn't know much about her, but I did notice the deference shown to her by the other local nationals.

The base held a ceremony to honor those and their families with longevity of service, and I had the privilege to attend as her commander. Afterward, on our walk back to the office, we shared a brief moment together. In her quiet tone she said, "Many commanders come and go, but few make a difference. Change slow if you want change to last." Who had time for slow? But she was right. For the local-nationals, who comprised a significant portion of our workforce, too much too soon would be patiently waited out till the next commander. The culture didn't get broken overnight, nor would it be transformed overnight. For the desired culture to endure, things couldn't be rushed or forced. A marginal approach was needed, and Chief had this figured out. For more than a year, I had a front row seat to his revolving door—a constant but patient trickle of feedback sessions, rebuke sessions, mentorship lessons, and guidance conducted in private. Marginally, step by step, airman after airman, Chief R helped restore a warrior spirit, organizational pride, and a sense of personal ownership and responsibility. Everyone was to bear their rightful share of known externalities, and they willingly did.

Chief R put in the hard work one tweak at a time, clarifying expectations, defining incentives, and driving accountability, always tying it back to our Air Force core values. Most of all, he tweaked hope back into the hearts of a broken culture—restoring the belief that they could and would be better than they were. Without his leadership, my urgent tone and vision as a commander would have fallen on deaf ears.

—

Our progress report to the wing commander was fast approaching when I heard a knock on the door. It was my young lieutenant asking us to

come downstairs to their work center. When Chief and I walked through
the customer lobby, it was empty. Then we entered the work center and
it was the same, empty. What did she want to show us?

Me: Where is everyone?

LT: Gone, sir. I sent them home early.

Chief: Early?

LT: Sir, we're fully caught up—documents processed, emails an-
swered, deadlines complete—we're all heading to the club if you want
to join.

CULTURE TAKING COMMAND

Mission accomplished—and in less than three months! A transformed
culture was underway and the change was palpable. What were the
signs? People wanted to come to work. They once again took pride in
their performance, in our mission, and in their dress and appearance.
Their attitudes were anything but apathetic. Accountability was happening at all levels, internally and across the base. Multiple solutions
were regularly being presented, and problems were getting resolved
before being elevated. Teams celebrated individuals and individuals celebrated the team. Innovation and ideas popped up everywhere
without anyone needing to be asked. Supervisors prioritized self-care
and substitutionary rest without stigma or fear of reprisal. And there
were fewer accusers and far more partners willing to bear their fair
share. As for my peers, they began to say hello at social gatherings
though no one coddled them. It was no longer about my boss and
those weekly updates. Nor was it about just me and Chief. It was a
transformed culture leading the way. With every step of success, the
tide shifted as waves of positive externalities started to roll in. Public
recognition, words of appreciation, and even Air-Force-level awards
started to happen. Internalization was becoming organic, and it was
beautiful to witness. Deep down, people wanted to excel, but they
needed an internalizer to lead the way—to create an environment
where standards and expectations were clear, where incentives were
credible, and where accountability ruled. An environment not too unlike my classroom.

—

Eighteen months and hundreds of internalizations later, the Pacific region announced Kadena as number one in almost every financial metric. Our budget staff would go on to win Best Financial Analysis Team of the Year. And my lieutenant? Top Junior Officer of the Year. But there was one externality that remained. I never forgot the young airman I met that first day. I found his duty location and asked his commander in Security Forces if I could take him out to lunch and invite him to the office. The airman didn't recognize me at first, but he complied with his commander's request. As we stood in that once-crowded lobby, which was now empty, I reminded him who I was and how we met. Then I thanked him for his patience and candid feedback. "I want you to know that the Air Force is better than what you saw that day. And I promise you, we'll try not to suck ever again." And we didn't.

CONCLUSION

Culture is powerful but responsive to change—collectively influenced yet individually engaged. Will you engage in culture's battle? People and organizations are "externality factories," producing positive and negative spillovers at alarming rates. What we collectively choose to accept and allow in the way of expectations, internalization, and accountability will shape our culture.

—

The official report from Afghanistan highlighted two compelling positive externalities. Amid the pervasive culture of complacency, there was still a vigilant remnant. It appeared the bomber was on his way to the larger event when he was unexpectedly approached and questioned by a group of soldiers. For a local-national to be without escort at that time of the morning was unauthorized. Under duress, the bomber likely panicked and prematurely self-detonated. The soldiers' vigilance and intervention prevented what might have been a far greater tragedy.

Medics and emergency personnel also remained vigilant. Their

urgent response and decisive actions not only saved lives but also pre-
vented a number of surviving patients from suffering greater bodily inju-
ries. In a culture that was permeated with negative externalities, there
stood a vigilant remnant that never let their guard down and, in turn,
poured protection over many. Culture had lost its way, but this remnant
did not, and their spillover was heroic. They answered the call when they
were needed most, internalizing that which they didn't cause, with five
brave souls bearing the ultimate cost. These were the leaders that day,
and for us, an eternal reminder that unless culture is challenged and
externalities are internalized, we will all pay a price we can ill afford.

CHAPTER 7

MARKET STRUCTURES AND POWER—BATTLE OF THE BRANDS

To each there comes in their lifetime a special moment when they are figuratively tapped on the shoulder and offered the chance to do a very special thing. . . . What a tragedy if that moment finds them unprepared or unqualified for that which could have been their finest hour.

—Sir Winston Churchill

BLUF: Helper or helpless? Defender or defenseless? Victor or victim? There will come various times and situations where convictions will be sorely tested. In these defining moments, what will be our leverage? In economics, power flows across the spectrum of market structures. One end possesses little to none, but at the other end, there's a strength that's undeniable. To battle and win when it matters most, we must persistently build toward that powerful end.

—

Chasing the American Dream never did unfold as my parents imagined. For forty years, it was one blue-collar business after the next. When I was ten, it was the season of Skokie Hardware, a small but densely packed store. I would tag along on "cement Saturdays" to help Mom and Dad replenish at the largest wholesaler in the Chicagoland area. Fellow shopkeepers would bull past each other through endless aisles of concrete floors, wooden pallets, and forklifts beeping at every turn. What you didn't see at the warehouse were women, but Mom wasn't intimidated. She navigated her way like a boss, checking off items while Dad filled two oversized carts. The final task was my time to shine: loading and unloading bags of cement. To hear mom say, "Dad needs your help" was always a pride-swelling privilege. Once we arrived at their store, Dad and I would pile the cement up and across, creating a bunker in the back. The reward for my labors was a haircut from the Greek barber next door and a burger from Hub's. And on the way home, Mom or Dad might slip me a ten. Cement Saturdays were good days.

On one occasion, while lying in the bunker, I heard loud voices coming from the front. I sneaked forward and saw two men arguing with Mom and Dad. They were returning used products, claiming they were damaged goods. This wasn't their first time. Mom decided enough was enough and refused the return. The men hurled insults, mocked her broken English, and spoke louder and faster than my parents could process. Towering over Mom, they demanded their money back and threatened to spread complaints across the community. I didn't quite understand it all, but the look on my parents' faces conveyed what was inaudible— disrespect, manipulation, injustice. These men were using their leverage of race, gender, and power to exploit and bully. I just stood and watched—scared, helpless, and defenseless. Were the threats credible? Would my parents lose their business? It was a regrettable moment, but sometimes the best regrets are served early.

LET'S PAUSE AND DISCUSS NONNEGOTIABLES

You know the saying "If you don't stand for something, you'll fall for anything." So what is it that we stand for—immovable, unwavering, ready to defend and fight? What are the nonnegotiables we insist upon in life and in leadership? The incident at my parents' hardware store left a lifelong, indelible mark. *Defend the defenseless, stare down injustice, and fight for the victim who has no voice, no power, and little to no leverage.* Nonnegotiables possess a strength of conviction far beyond the ebb and flow of preferences and opinions. They center upon principles, ideals, core values, and beliefs. They're the causes for which we will fall on our leadership sword, burn bridges, and enter into harm's way, knowingly and willingly, to support and defend. Nonnegotiables hold to certain truths and inalienable rights and follow a code of honor and ethics. To turn a blind eye to them would be to abandon conscience and risk lasting regret.

Somewhere in our transformative journey, I hope we see with absolute clarity and conviction that leadership is about far more than measurable results, material successes, and fleeting praise. It's what we do with all those things that matters. More important than any wealth is what we do with those resources. More important than a noteworthy reputation is what we do with our credibility. And more important than a promotion or position is what we do with our elevated platform. If we use the material blessings of leadership merely to generate more material blessings, then we've missed the point, and as leaders we're most to be pitied. We've reduced our high calling to just another self-serving pursuit. But if we can see and value our leadership in the light of nonnegotiables, then as Sir Winston Churchill so eloquently stated, we may indeed find ourselves qualified and ready for that special moment, our finest hour. When all is said and done, we want to know that our leadership, and all that was invested in it, stood for something beyond ourselves, firmly planted on the right side of conscience and history. If we're to meet such a calling, our leadership needs leverage.

Note: Nonnegotiables may evolve, and that's OK. We may often find ourselves in the ebb and flow of "gray," where compromise, give-and-take, and flexibility are the golden rule. Making concessions may not be easy or preferred, but depending on our situation and end goal, it may be exactly what we need to be doing. Traits like flexibility serve us well in negotiations, or help us gain consensus and move the agenda forward. Gray may also be "gracious," giving room to reassess, change, or reaffirm what is or isn't truly black and white. Things we once tolerated, even advocated for, may later appear unacceptable. And that which we once deemed intolerable may gradually be viewed as preferential. Life has a way of presenting moral dilemmas where sometimes nonnegotiables conflict and a choice must be made. It serves notice that not all personal convictions are created equal. Gray offers the time and space we need to self-discover and to realize our clearest nonnegotiables, and that's a good thing.

MORE THAN JUST MONOPOLY—MARKET STRUCTURE AND MARKET POWER

Before majoring in economics, I majored in Monopoly, my favorite childhood board game. It begins at one end of the market spectrum, known as *perfect competition*, and concludes at the other end, known as *monopoly.* Under perfect competition there are no barriers to entry and no differentiating leverage. Everyone begins with the same funding, the same rules, and the same opportunity to win. With a little strategy and a lucky roll, players acquire properties and negotiate deals to outmaneuver their competition. Over time, a separation in assets and wealth begins to take hold where some become price takers and others, price influencers. No longer is the playing field equal; instead it is dictated by the influencers, till eventually the entire market gets engulfed by one player, the *monopolist.* The principle is clear: Accumulate assets and build wealth to rise above, to differentiate, and to leverage market power. That's how we influence the outcome. Perhaps not exactly how the real world plays out, but it's not far off.

In between perfect competition and monopoly we discover the broader market structure known as *monopolistic competition.* It's where the majority of the game is played, as competitors strive to differentiate and rise above the crowd. Ironically, the game's purpose and goal have been replicated by the real-life brand.

The Power of Branding

For nearly ninety years, competitive branding has defined Monopoly's sustained journey. Consider that there are more than fifteen hundred versions translated into forty-seven languages across 115 countries. With more than 300 million copies sold and over 1.5 billion people who have played, the brand has never stopped growing and expanding its market share and market power. The game has been showcased in national tournaments and world championships, has been featured in movies and video games, and continues to reinvent itself with every generation. Who else can boast such an assortment of collector's editions, special editions, and ten anniversary editions, each eliciting nostalgic memories? More than just a game, it has become a permanent household member, connecting family and friends, communities young and old, all under a familiar bond. Other than ancient classics like chess and checkers, no game has achieved a loyal following and brand status quite like Monopoly. The game may never attain the status of a pure monopoly, but in a crowded field, its longevity and worldwide popularity more than speak to a winning formula. Monopoly may be its name, but competitive branding has been its ceaselessly powerful game.

"C's" Your Brand to Seize Market Power

Most of us begin our leadership journey like we do in the game, on the same ground floor with little to no leverage. But with a little strategy and a lot of effort, we can begin to separate from the crowd. It doesn't require unique talents or a special endowment to rise above, but it does take focus and commitment to build a brand that stands apart. At everyone's disposal are six C's that can elevate a brand and help it seize market power: Competency, Craftsmanship, Character, Credibility, Cause, and Compass. When we build these, we'll be ready to go toe to toe with anyone and come away victorious.

Competency and craftsmanship. These showcase our brand's relevance and quality. They're a leader's bread and butter, the basic building blocks that visibly and tangibly shout, "You need me!" *Competency* embodies knowledge and expertise, but it's never a static pursuit. Rather, competency's endeavor is maximizing value by remaining relevant to meet present and future needs. For this reason, competency maintains an attentive posture, one that is current, curious, and creative. The more personalized and thoughtful our insight, the greater our leverage will be.

Craftsmanship is quality marked by a heightened level of care and attention to detail. There should be a "pride of ownership" that gets stamped on every seal of approval, as it directly reflects your brand. For leaders, this is most evident in their organizations. The people, their attitudes and performance, the quality of products and services, and the overall culture—every strength and weakness is on display for all to see and either elevates or discredits the craftsmanship. A leader's brand loses substantive value when their organization has obvious cracks. The two, the leader and their organization, are inseparable, and only a unified excellence will do. Therefore, pursue quality across your organization holistically, so that craftsmanship becomes a collective stamp of approval.

Character and credibility. These are what keep people coming back. Together, they convey, "You can trust and rely on me." If competency and craftsmanship are a leader's bread and butter, then character and credibility must be the main course. *Character* encompasses moral attributes as demonstrated by one's behavior. It's judged by consistency: Is there alignment in what we say and do? Are our decisions and priorities congruent with our convictions, values, and beliefs? Whether at home or at work, in the presence of others or alone, character exudes steadfast integrity. It's not for others, but for ourselves—so we can look in the mirror and respect who we see. That said, strength of character doesn't mean moral perfection. If it did, which of us could pass that test? Rather, character's hallmark is moral reflection followed by action. As humanity is led by humility, character resolves to acknowledge failures, seek forgiveness, and rise after every fall. To leverage the conscience of others, we must grow in character. For therein lies a moral authority that transcends any formal or positional authority that we and others might possess.

Credibility is character's reputation developed over time and carries the weight of words like *reliable*, *dependable*, and *trustworthy*. It's what earns autonomy and is the basis for network capital, where people will confidently and joyfully put their names on the line for us and on our behalf. Credibility may take years to establish, but only seconds to destroy. It's weighty yet fragile, and where character is jeopardized, credibility isn't far behind. It's a sober reminder to think twice before breaking with character, and it's why we must keep our word and aim to follow through even when that's painful. Competency and craftsmanship may catch the eye, but character and credibility are what sustain a lasting brand loyalty. Credibility is character's priceless reward. Once earned, it's a source of leverage worth protecting at all costs.

Cause and compass. This is what drives us to create the bread and butter and the main course day in and day out. It's the heart, the vision, the mission, the reason why we aim to keep being the best. It's also what elevates our presentation—the decor, the service, the atmosphere, all that Michelin planning. It's not peripheral, but rather a central byproduct of our cause and compass. The other C's turn good into great, but cause and compass turn great into something unique and memorable. They draw upon the senses, stirring an emotional response. Having experienced wonder, hearts whisper, "What drives this place? Who's the founder, the owner, the leader? How did they get started and what does their future hold? Please tell us your story."

Cause is our story. It's how we forge an intimate bond with the audience. It's our personal journey of discovering an idea that becomes our ideal. It's why we endure and sacrifice, and more than an appeal to conscience, it's our appeal to hearts and imaginations to consider what could be. Cause is the inspiration of our leadership and our leverage into the soul of others. We must refine our story and message it well, for no good brand should be without a compelling story.

Compass is the guide providing clarity and forward direction to our cause. Every vision needs a definitive path to follow; otherwise it will likely remain just a dream. Compass carries both a strategic and a moral element. Strategic is about thinking through the steps and developing the necessary plans to execute milestones. It relies on a network of partners and investors to support and strengthen the cause. Moral keeps us on the straight and narrow so we don't divert or digress from the other C's, or from our nonnegotiables, especially in times of trial. Moral is our North Star that keeps us from compromising in areas that might win us the battle but lose us the war. *Every cause needs a compass.* Without clear signposts, no matter how compelling our story, listeners won't know where or how to follow.

ONE TEAM, ONE FIGHT . . . BUT TWO BRANDS?

During the height of America's conflict in the Middle East, a primary hub for airlift was Charleston Air Force Base, in South Carolina. Movement of personnel and wartime assets was happening around the clock, and it was the close partnership between the active-duty and reserve forces that made it happen. Reservists were Charleston's long-standing "weekend warriors." They maintained full-time civilian jobs while dedicating one weekend a month for military training and prepa-ration. On the surface, the two forces were indistinguishable. Both wore the same uniform, recited the same core values, and performed similar duties to accomplish our shared wartime mission. But beyond this, the contrast in leadership, culture, and attitudes was stark.

It was the difference between full time versus part time, every day versus weekends, and performing the duty versus training for duty. The active were 24/7/365 and deployable at a moment's notice, whereas the reserves had the freedom and flexibility to hold civilian careers. And while the active force generally moved every few years, reservists could remain in place indefinitely. Some at Charleston held working relation-ships that were decades long. More seasoned in age and experience, the reservists possessed a deeper familiarity with one another and with or-ganizations across the base. In this respect, the reserves provided sta-bility and a level of continuity that proved invaluable to our nation's mission. We were truly one team, one fight, but two distinctly different cultures serving side by side for a common cause.

—

On this particular weekend, a large group of reservists were about to conduct a "flyaway" exercise—a dress rehearsal of sorts. They would travel to an alternate location, perform operations as though they were deployed, then return a few days later to resume their civilian lives. Following an exercise, reservists would flood our building to file paperwork for their pay and reimbursements. Many had to travel long distances to come to Charleston, so going back and forth was both burdensome and time consuming for our reservists. One of my airmen decided to come to the rescue. He volunteered his weekend to collect and audit the documents immediately upon their return from the flyaway exercise, thus saving the reservists the extra round trip. His going above and beyond didn't surprise anyone. My airman was one of Charleston's best and brightest, our Junior Airman of the Year. He may have been young and still growing in experience, but his competitive brand already stood apart. His dedication, work ethic, and positive attitude were second to none. Everyone on the team appreciated his efforts, including customers across the base. I would receive feedback every week praising him by name. He exemplified competency and craftsmanship, character and credibility, and his excellence reflected kindly on both the organization and me. My airman loved the Air Force and had great pride in serving his fellow warriors. Nothing could dissuade him from coming in this weekend to serve, because providing unmatched customer service was his nonnegotiable.

The reservists that day numbered over 150 personnel. Together with his supervisor, a young lieutenant, my airman prepared the paperwork in advance and entered the reception center ready to expedite the process. Less than an hour and it would all be over, claims completed and no need for a return visit. But the restless, haggard audience was hardly in the mood. Many stood in the back, anxiously waiting to depart. Amid the grumbling, diminishing returns suddenly took an unspeakable turn. The ranking reservist, a lieutenant colonel, and his top enlisted aide crumpled their paperwork and hurled it at my airman's face while saying aloud, "This is bullshit. We're tired, and we're going home." As they stormed out, the entire crowd abruptly followed suit, 150 reservists wadding up their papers and throwing them across the room. My airman stood stunned . . . speechless . . . helpless. The two ranking reservists leveraged their power in the worst way. Instead of asserting calm, they abused their position and authority to behave however they wanted, throwing fuel on the fire. Their actions mocked and publicly humiliated the youngest, most defenseless person in the room and incited the disgruntled crowd. There was nothing my airman could say or do in that moment to save himself.

At home that Sunday afternoon, I received a panicked call from the lieutenant, asking for my immediate presence. By the time I arrived, the reception center was empty except for the papers that were scattered everywhere. On the far side of the room sat my airman, alone and staring down with hands over his head. I pulled up a chair next to him, but he wouldn't look at me. Slowly he unraveled all that happened and likened it to "getting spit in the face" but not being allowed to respond. And thank God he didn't. Any physical retaliation by his six-feet, four-inch, 250-pound frame would not have ended well. Instead he absorbed the full blow of indignity without a word. Finally he looked up, his bloodshot eyes revealing raw emotions. "Sir, how can anyone wearing the same uniform, with the same core values . . . do this? How could they treat me this way? I just wanted to help." I felt his pain and anger. I knew his shame and disappointment. It was "cement Saturday" all over again, as our hearts sank together.

A BRAND DAMAGED

In the blink of an eye, the reserve brand, their character and credibility, and the notion of "one team, one fight" was crushed. The Air Force brand was also jeopardized. My airman saw only one uniform, and that uniform betrayed him. Before parting ways, with voice trembling, he said, "Sir, this isn't the Air Force I joined. My reenlistment is coming up, but I won't be staying." The disillusionment he faced seemed irreparable, as though nothing could erase the stain. I apologized for what had happened and told him not to make his decision based on this one incident. I assured him, "They will be held accountable."

No matter how tired they may have been, what happened was inexcusable and demanded internalization. Anything less would have sent a message condoning their behavior. And that wouldn't have been the Air Force I had joined either. A price had to be exacted, and the rightful parties needed to bear the cost. I was ready to apply whatever leverage necessary to achieve the results I needed. It wasn't about retribution. It was about restorative justice—confronting the reservists so that they might do the right thing. It was about recovering whatever faith my airman had left in the Air Force and its core values. I wasn't sure what the outcome would be, but I was certain of this: A nonnegotiable had been violated, and my airman wasn't leaving the Air Force without a fight.

—

I called my boss, the active-duty wing commander, and told him what had happened and what I believed needed to be done. He and the reserve commander were peers and personal friends, so I had my concerns. But I wasn't seeking permission. I was providing him a professional courtesy so he wouldn't be blindsided. I was prepared to respectfully disagree if he advised to the contrary. Fortunately, this didn't happen. My organization and I had established the brand excellence necessary to leverage his professional, if not personal, support. I then pulled from a broad network of relationships to bolster my insights and guidance. Both Legal and HR provided sound protection and wisdom regarding what was judicially and administratively appropriate. And then I contacted the reserve headquarters and requested a meeting with the reserve commander. He was superior to me in rank and position but fell outside my chain of command. Hence our relationship was more collegial than authoritative. In fact, at every engagement, he called me by my first name and made it a point to always thank me for my team's outstanding support to his members. For financial matters, we were the only game in town—any issues had to come through us for resolution. I guess you could say we possessed a local monopoly. He recognized our indispensable craftsmanship and the importance of our competency in serving their financial needs. I suppose that's why he would regularly conclude our conversations with "Don't hesitate if you ever need me for anything." Little did we realize it would be for this cause.

A BRAND ESTABLISHED

My airman may have been the best, but our entire organization had established a reputation of excellence across the base and with our

Air Mobility headquarters. We were known for outstanding customer service and support, for bending over backward to meet every mission need. We were a quiet bunch but extremely proud of our mission and the contributions we were making to the warfighter. Leaders across Charleston, including the reserve leadership, knew our importance and esteemed our reliable and competent service. It paved the way for credibility up and down the chain, and everywhere I went I heard "Thank you. We appreciate your team." Having a network of support that was strong and broad proved invaluable as I stood my ground, especially with the reserves who had more longevity and seniority on base. Facing situations of "he said, she said" often came down to brand strength, so this was my confidence heading into the fire. With my lieutenant as a witness, we drove to their headquarters.

—

To my surprise, the commander's entire leadership team was assembled and standing behind his desk. I thought to myself, if it looks and smells like an ambush, it probably is. After a brief welcome, I was given the floor. As calmly as possible, I stated the facts—every egregious word and deed. I listed the names and ranks of the two primary instigators and also four others who were identified as having made derogatory comments. After handing over the official statements and eyewitness accounts, I concluded with two nonnegotiable requests: first, that each of the six members individually apologize to my airman in person; and second, that disciplinary actions be swift and commensurate. I also asked that the specific measures be delivered to me in writing.

News of the incident had spread throughout my organization and everyone was outraged. To prevent further escalation, I advised the commander that no reservist should approach my team for assistance until after this matter was resolved. Unlike our previous encounters, my first name disappeared. It was all business, as indicated by his direct tone. "Major Paik, my staff will conduct a thorough review, and once we've gathered all sides of the story, I will decide the way forward." He had clearly been prepped. "And as for our members needing assistance, you will make sure your people do their duty."

POSITIONAL AUTHORITY VERSUS MORAL AUTHORITY

His response was cold and calculated, empty of any sympathy or concern for my airman, *our* airman. Perhaps I shouldn't have been surprised, but I was. The reserve commander may have held formal and positional authority, and even his way forward may have been procedurally correct, but none of that mattered to me. What most caught my attention was his lack of compassion for my airman. His no-nonsense response was devoid of any personal remorse or urgency. He instead placed his demands on me to continue serving his members. This was the epitome of positional leverage. After he spoke his last word, he leaned back in his chair as if to say, "It's time to leave."

My lieutenant took his cue to exit and turned toward the door, but I stood immovable. The reserve commander may have had the rank and position, but I had the moral authority. I wasn't sure how to respond or what would happen next, but I refused to leave on those terms. I once heard someone say regarding leadership, "Unless you're willing to be fired, you're not worthy of the position." I'd never quite understood the depth of what that meant until now. Sometimes in life and in leadership, it's time to burn the bridge and leverage it all for what's right.

SIR, WITH ALL DUE RESPECT . . .

In the military, there's no better way to begin when you're about to unleash. To summarize, I followed with this: "My airman insisted on working this weekend, giving up time with his family because he wanted to help your team. But instead of being thanked, he was bullied and publicly humiliated by several of your leaders—the very ones who should have supported him. It's all in the written statements. As a result, one of the most dedicated young airmen you'll ever meet no longer wants anything to do with 'our' Air Force, and for now doesn't plan to reenlist. Sir, we cannot allow that to happen." I had made my cause clear. But I wasn't finished.

"No one in my organization has ever needed to come to your orga-nization for help, but I see your people in my building every day need-ing our assistance. Sir, I've held your leadership in the highest regard, as you've always thanked and praised my team and offered help when needed. Now is the time. I need their apologies and disciplinary actions today." A compass was provided.

In other words, unless you address my nonnegotiables, "No soup for you!" I turned to the door and dropped the mic.

BRAND VERSUS BRAND

Positional authority versus moral authority. Bureaucratic procedures battling cause and compass. I appealed to our core values, character, and credibility. I reminded the reserve commander of our organiza-tion's relevance and craftsmanship, and his own words of praise and assistance. I relied on my network capital and reemphasized what was at stake. In short, I was letting him know that his leadership brand, the reputation of the reserve force, and the core values of our Air Force were on the line. When you're confident in the strength of your brand, it lends courage to fight for your nonnegotiables with anyone.

—

As we departed the building, my lieutenant whispered, "Sir, that was awesome!" And it was. Later that afternoon, I had six reservists in my office offering their apology to my young airman. At that moment, their actions, more than their sincerity, were what mattered. And by email, I received their respective consequences. The punishments were swift and severe, as none remained in uniform very long thereafter. The reserve commander had listened to my cause and followed my compass. And in doing so, he salvaged his brand and our relationship. Most important, his actions restored my airman's faith. Two weeks later he reenlisted and continued to serve in the Air Force he loved.

Nine years had passed when I received an email with an attached news article. It was from my airman, who was back in Charleston, being publicly recognized by his current base as their Senior Enlisted

Leader of the Year, and still going strong on active duty—serving, inspiring, and bringing his brand of unmatched customer service to others. In the interview, he was asked, "Who was your greatest leadership influence?" Highlighted in yellow was his answer: "My commander from Charleston."

CONCLUSION

Dad opened the register, handed the men their cash, and told them to never come back. As they walked out with victory in hand, I feared how their threats would undo our little store. My parents seemingly had no leverage. They lacked English skills, didn't understand the cultural nuances, and faced stiff competition from big-box stores nearby. But they survived, and did so on their own terms, for nearly fifteen years.

—

Do you know your nonnegotiables, and are you leveraged to fight for them and win? My parents were never taught how to "differentiate" above the competitive crowd, nor were they given lessons on strengthening their brand. But that's exactly what they did during their years in business. Day in and day out, Skokie Hardware provided a level of quality, expertise, and service that was unmatched, constantly proving their competency and worth. Whether they were making keys, fixing window screens, or leading customers to the right nuts and bolts, their craftsmanship came with personalized care and attention to detail. Mom and Dad knew their customers by name, along with their stories. They extended credit based on trust without charging interest, and showed grace in times of need. Snow, rain, or shine, their day-in, day-out consistency and faithful adherence to commitments earned a level of trust, respect, and credibility across their customer base and from local businesses. When the moment of crisis came, their brand stood strong and their cause remained resilient. Fairness, justice, dignity, and respect belonged to everyone, no matter their life position or status.

Over the years, with every small business that followed, Mom and

Dad carved a similar path of competency, craftsmanship, character, and credibility, always having their story to share and a North Star to guide them. They never achieved the wealth of a monopoly, but they earned the priceless wealth of a loyal community and the admiration and respect of their children and grandchildren.

That fateful day, on the drive home, Dad tried slipping me a ten, but I refused. I didn't want it. I'd been paid with a life lesson that's proven far more valuable: Build and strengthen your leadership brand, for it's your monopoly power to do good.

CHAPTER 8

RISK VERSUS REWARD— THE ULTIMATE COVERAGE

Only those who will risk going too far can possibly find out how far one can go.

—T. S. Eliot

BLUF: No risk, no return. Big risk, big return. What seems a straightforward proposition is hardly straightforward in application. Risk hits a nerve that makes us instinctively pull back. But there are times and situations where we need to embolden others to move the needle forward. The courage to take risks can't be borrowed, but it can be covered. Risk isn't solely an aversion to be managed and feared; it's an opportunity for us to cover and lead.

—

In the fall of 1999, I was stationed at Osan Air Base and excited to explore South Korea at every opportunity. My ride was an old Daewoo sedan, for which I paid $500 to an outgoing soldier. It was a beater, but sturdy and decent sized. Best of all, it was cheap to insure. One weekend my wife and I, along with two of our friends, decided to enjoy a Korean barbecue on the outskirts of town. By the time we finished, *it was pitch-black outside, making it difficult to see the road. While waiting at a T intersection, I had to watch four lanes of oncoming traffic, two going one direction and two going the other. At the first decent opening, I punched the accelerator and turned left, full speed ahead. What I couldn't see was the person standing on the narrow median, trying to cross. They were holding a bag of groceries and stepped directly into my path. The thud resounded, my wife screamed, and loud gasps came from the back seat. Writhing on the ground was an elderly woman. I instinctively picked her up and placed her in the car and we rushed to a nearby hospital. She was whisked away by emergency personnel as we were met by two administrators. They knew just enough English and we knew just enough Korean. They asked about our relationship to the patient. Were we her children? No. Grandchildren? No. Niece? Nephew? Friend? No, no, and no. They appeared confused before I finally responded, "I'm the person who hit her." Confusion turned to shock. Amid severe lawsuits and a climb in uninsured motorists, hit-and-runs had become the country's norm. After giving a statement to the police, we were advised to contact our insurance company and depart before her family members arrived.*

It was the middle of the night, but a representative from USAA insurance answered my call. I was bracing for the worst. Would we get sued? How would I pay the medical bills? And, God forbid, what would happen if the woman didn't recover? I should've never bought a car or driven in Korea. *Would I have enough coverage? The representative asked several questions, mostly to ensure that we were OK. If there were deficiencies with our inexpensive policy, nothing was mentioned. Rather, it was one reassurance after the next. Before I could list my many concerns, the rep ended with a broad statement of confidence. "You have nothing to worry about. We'll take it from here. Captain Paik, we've got you covered." And to my amazement . . . they did.*

DON'T JUST MANAGE RISK—LEAD IT

Insurance companies are in the business of managing risk, but at that moment, USAA communicated leadership. It's what enabled me to get back on the road, to risk once again, and to continue traveling around Korea without fear or reservation. As a company, USAA had done their "managing" homework. They knew the risks of driving in and around Seoul, with its ten million people. They knew better than anyone the habits and potential accidents their members faced. Therefore they knew exactly what liability and collision coverages were needed. I had no idea what my policy did or didn't cover, but at that moment, what I knew didn't matter. What mattered was that they knew me and backed me with the full strength of their brand. In doing so, USAA led a much greater purpose with their coverage, "serving those who serve." That night, the rep compassionately listened and confidently reassured me. But more importantly, they followed through with their promised coverage, not only taking care of me but taking care of the woman who got hit, her family's concerns, and any resulting consequences. No mention of premiums, deductibles, accident history, or any prohibitive fine print. It was total backing and no backtracking. I never heard another word about the incident other than news from the hospital that the woman was going to be OK.

Managing risk places fear and mitigation onto center stage. The focus becomes probabilities, severities, and potential consequences, with the threat of imminent failure. Data and stats, equations and calculations, plans and strategies are all aimed at minimizing this constantly lurking, complex nemesis. But in leading risk, the paradigm gets flipped. We don't see an antagonist to be avoided; we see a superpower to be unleashed. It shouts opportunities and offers possibilities that squash our anxieties and fears. And so we no longer avoid risk at all costs. Instead we come to a place of needing it, seeking it, and welcoming it, not merely with words or blind bravado, but through the full coverage of our leadership brand. This is how we give courage to risk. There are plenty of worthy professions dedicated to managing risk, but our calling is to lead it. As leaders, we're the insurance policy, the provider, and the underwriter all in one. And there should be no prohibitive fine print when things get messy. We're the top cover that frees our people to risk and risk big. We appreciate the lawyer's and the manager's legal and statistical caution, but we never settle there. The final word resides with the leaders of risk, and it's for a reward that's worth our cover.

LEADING RISK—COVERING THE MESS

While in Japan, I had a young lieutenant who was an absolute spitfire—enthusiastic, intelligent, relational, ambitious, and full of ideas. She had the right insight, but she sat frozen without top cover. One attribute was decisively missing: being a leader of risk. Playing it safe became her default position, and the mission suffered as a result. In our first formal feedback meeting, I handed her the official Air Force document with just two handwritten words: "GO CRAZY!" She sat confused. I knew this was her first leadership position, so I offered some marginal feedback. I expected her to move the mission forward and do the things necessary to take care of her people, with or without my permission. This would require taking risky steps and leading risk for others. But I assured her, whatever blame or failure came as a result, "I've got your back. Go crazy!" She smiled and responded, "Yes, sir."

When I arrived at my office the next morning, my voice messages and emails were overflowing. I hit play to the sound of one irate leader after the next: "Lieutenant Colonel Paik, this is unacceptable." "Seung, how come I'm just seeing this now?" "Call me . . . it's about that email." I scrolled through my inbox and saw the repeated subject line: "Government Travel Card Delinquencies, A Leadership Problem." The no-reply email was addressed to all Kadena commanders, chiefs, and first sergeants, basically the entire base leadership. And the message began, "Ladies and Gentlemen, we have a leadership problem." The author? My young lieutenant. I was mortified.

The week prior, during a team meeting, I had declared in no uncertain terms that the base's travel-card problem, with its high number of delinquencies, was a direct reflection of poor leadership: "If leaders and supervisors held their people accountable, we wouldn't be in this mess." She heard that and decided to run with it. The email's tone was direct and authoritative, and the attached spreadsheet contained content that was detailed and brutally transparent. It aired every organization's dirty laundry, highlighting the most delinquent accounts by name, including names of base leaders. All laid bare for the world to see. She highlighted Kadena's last-place ranking, and concluded her message with a harsh guarantee that unless leaders took this seriously, we would surely fail the upcoming audit.

She didn't just go crazy—she went ballistic. How would I overcome this? How would I show my face at the next leaders meeting? I called the lieutenant into my office and stood her at attention while I gave her a piece of my mind. "How could you be so careless! What were you think-ing? Why didn't you run this past me? Do you have any idea how many leaders you blindsided and how much damage control I now have to do? I trusted you, and you blew it. Grab your belongings and go. You're fired!"

BEARING AND REPAIRING THE MESS

Top cover means covering your people, not covering your butt. Owning and internalizing the risks of others is dangerous business but par for the course. We should expect painful unknowns and messy failures. In leading risk, bearing and repairing is what gives our coverage cred-ibility. Anything less would be hypocritical.

So no, I didn't fire her or say any of those harsh words. If I had, my feedback would have meant nothing and I never could have con-vinced her to step out and take risk again. Could she have used better judgment and a softer tone? Of course. Did I empower her too soon? Perhaps. But at the end of the day, my lieutenant simply repeated my words and did what I'd asked in trying to fulfill our mission, just not how I had envisioned. The facts were accurate and the guidance was crystal clear. Other than a little feedback on email etiquette, I reaf-firmed her actions and applauded the risk. There was no point in dis-cussing the voice messages and emails, nor the triage that lay ahead. That was fine print she didn't need to hear, as it would only diminish the promise of having full coverage. Covering the risk meant covering the mess. The haters could take it up with me, but not with her.

—

One by one, I contacted each leader, listened to their frustrations, and apologized accordingly. But once the vent was over, I simply asked,

"Was there anything in the email that was inaccurate or unclear?" There wasn't a single rebuttal. In essence, my lieutenant nailed it. Her "crazy" email created the firestorm we needed to get the solution rolling.

The base commander read her email and followed up with a message of his own, reemphasizing my lieutenant's words and demanding immediate improvements. My top cover now had his ultimate cover. A problem that had persisted for years was resolved in months, and our base became the model for improvement. If only the Air Force knew that the prescriptive solution resided in two words: "GO CRAZY."

REMEMBERING THAT RISK IS A LEARNED BEHAVIOR

As mentioned before, we all have a built-in aversion to risk, and therefore staying on the sidelines is our natural inclination. And the longer we stay there, the more improbable it becomes to jump on the field, especially as the stakes grow higher. But we can't teach and learn risk-taking behavior from the sidelines. It has to be experienced, failure and all, out on the field early and often.

Sure, I could have waited longer before empowering my lieutenant to go crazy, but how long? There's no limit to the amount of assured safety we all crave. We have to assess the person being empowered and the potential reward that's at stake, then decide: sidelines or playing field? If playing field, have we prepared them for success? And if sidelines, what's holding us back? For it is the leader's natural inclination as well. What my team did was important but not life-threatening. No one was going to die from our risky business. We could afford to go crazy and deal with the unforeseen mess—it's the opposite that we couldn't afford. As leaders, we model risk by sending, entrusting, empowering, and then covering. We model it by battling self-preservation and the false comfort of control. And we model it by taking full ownership of whatever the outcome is. When we willingly cover risk and its mess, we can experience the reward of "aversion conversion." It's where control is replaced by coverage, fear is exchanged for opportunity, and risk is embraced as the new norm. When we empower our people with top cover that holds water, they will attempt to walk on water. My greatest problem going forward wasn't getting my lieutenant off the sidelines, but trying to rein her in on the playing field—the best mess any leader could ask for.

Note: This once risk-averse lieutenant went all-in with a major career change and pursued her dream to be an Arab linguist, later becoming a military attaché in Egypt—all while becoming a wife and mom, and adding a cryptocurrency side gig. Not bad for a person who used to "play it safe."

LEADING RISK—COVERING THE SHAME

The more we have, the more protective we become.

—

What an incredible year it was, going from worst to first. The team worked their tails off to regain a level of trust and respect, achieving a number of awards and accolades along the way. It was a time for celebration, and it coincided perfectly with our end-of-year holiday party in downtown Okinawa. Spearheading the event was my second-in-command, my captain. After returning from Afghanistan the year prior, he'd wasted no time making an impact across the base and the organization. My captain was a budding star in our field, a shoo-in for promotion, and the recipient of a prestigious internship with Microsoft. His future was bright and his reputation firmly established. As the evening's formal program came to a close, the karaoke began . . . our cue to exit. I turned things over to my captain and departed with a deep sense of joy and satisfaction. The party continued late into the night, and they earned every minute.

It was after 3:00 a.m. when I was awakened by the police. My star had been arrested and taken into custody by Japanese authorities. A Breathalyzer test revealed that he had exceeded the legal alcohol limit after an eyewitness linked him to a hit-and-run in the parking lot. As his commander, I was allowed into the detention area, where we could speak through a barricade, patrolled by an armed guard. The scene

*was surreal. I could hardly believe that just hours before, we were cel-
ebrating . . . and now he was behind bars. My captain assured me that
it was either mistaken identity or a misunderstanding. That there was
no hit-and-run and that he didn't drive during or after the party. As for
the Breathalyzer, it was administered as he stepped out of the party, not
out of a vehicle. Relieved, I immediately shared his testimony with the
authorities and asked for his release. But they calmly held to the accu-
sation and the eyewitness testimony, and recited the standard proce-
dure: mandatory ten-day confinement before facing a judge, or sooner
should the accused confess.*

*Later that morning, I met with my boss, the base commander, and
conveyed all that had happened. He had already been made aware.
"Are you sure?" he asked. "One hundred percent," I assured him. To
secure his release, we would need to document our justification and
coordinate approval through our headquarters in Tokyo. The base
commander reminded me that "our" credibility was on the line at the
highest levels. I understood. I contacted a friend in the Office of Special
Investigations because of their close partnership with the local authorities. He expressed caution. "Seung, in my experience, they don't
detain our military without hard evidence. I'm pretty sure they have
more than just an eyewitness." If that were the case, I responded, why
didn't the authorities just say so? "Because they're giving the member
an opportunity to confess." The following day, my friend confirmed—
video cameras were mounted atop the light poles across the parking
lot. I called my commander and asked him to refrain from sending the
request. I needed one more gut check from my captain.*

*With each passing day, my captain's bearings noticeably deterio-
rated. As we sat in the detention center, I offered once more, "Is there
anything from that night you may have missed? Any additional details
that might help with our justification?" He repeated the same story and
again confirmed his innocence, but this time his tone and demeanor
were different. With the Breathalyzer, the eyewitness account, the cameras, and the word of caution from my friend, my doubts were piling
high, but my captain gave me his word and said he was innocent. So
I stuck by his side even if it meant bearing a resulting shame. I told
him how much I appreciated his courage and integrity, how proud I
was of him, and that the wing commander and I were doing everything*

possible to secure his release. As I stood up to leave, I could see he was distraught. I could tell there was something he desperately wanted to say.

And then, it happened. He confessed. "Sir, I did it. As I backed out in the parking lot, I hit the car behind me. I panicked and reparked, then ran inside thinking no one noticed. But when I came back out, the authorities were waiting. That's when they took my Breathalyzer." As he paused, I felt a sense of relief but also my own shame for having proclaimed his innocence to everyone, especially to my wing commander. He continued. "I haven't been able to eat or sleep. It's been killing me knowing that you're covering my lie and putting your name on the line. I was afraid of losing everything, but I don't care anymore. I just want to tell the truth and take whatever comes. Boss, I'm so sorry."

—

There was no condoning or excusing his reckless behavior and the dishonesty that followed. My captain's crime was a serious offense that could have resulted in damages and consequences far worse than a dented fender. He was wrong, he failed, and he deserved every bit of punishment that was to follow. But there was also shame on my part for believing his lies and trusting my emotional bias more than the objective evidence that had been presented. In doing so, I irrationally and unfavorably questioned and scrutinized another country's culture and justice system. I jeopardized my credibility and risked the credibility of my chain of command. Nevertheless, I'm not ashamed to reveal this story, because this is exactly what leading risk is about—taking full ownership of the dangers at hand. Sometimes it means covering the mess, and sometimes it means covering the shame.

COVERING THE SHAME, EVEN TO OUR SHAME

There's great risk in covering shame—perhaps the greatest risk we'll take. It's giving up our name for the sake of another. I understood my captain's panic. He had so much going for him, so much to protect personally and professionally. And then suddenly, in a moment of reckless judgment, he had everything to lose. Safety appeared behind the lies, and there he immediately ran and hid, exchanging the truth for those lies and giving away his most precious asset, his integrity. It would take a hefty price with great peril to get it back, for him to step out in truth, to confess, and to bear the shame and all the consequences to follow. The risk became far too much until . . . he could see someone who was willing to stand beside him. Someone who would bear the risk and outcome together. Someone who would sacrifice their name to defend his name, offer their reputation to protect his reputation, and bear judgment to declare his innocence. This is what it meant to cover his shame. The only question was, Would the recipient respond in a manner worthy of my risk? Leading risk meant bearing the shame, but risking the unknown.

Perhaps it was foolish in the world's eyes, putting my name on the line for someone who may not be deserving or may continue to act in an unworthy manner. But it's the risk required to authentically convey this message: I'm placing your restoration above my reputation. I wasn't sure if he was or wasn't innocent. And I didn't know if he would or wouldn't confess. All I knew was that I felt called to walk alongside him even to my shame, and to risk my name because of his word. And that was the conviction and courage he needed to step out of hiding and risk it all to reclaim his integrity. It was the ultimate risk reward.

—

I went directly to my commander's office and apologized. I told him my captain had confessed. Thankfully, the request for release had not been routed, and to this day I wonder if he had inside intel. He graciously accepted my apology and requested an update with the forthcoming consequences. The list was long. I removed my captain from his leadership position, docked his pay, canceled his medal, lined out his promotion recommendation, and took away his internship. He received fines for his off-base conduct, his car was impounded, and he had no driving privileges for six months. It was a scarlet letter. Professionally, he lost everything except the opportunity to remain in the Air Force and regain our trust. And for that, he was grateful.

COVERING DOESN'T "COVER UP"

Covering acknowledges and accepts the shame, whereas covering up avoids or rejects it. Leaders who cover up are ashamed of shame. They disassociate from, dismiss, and distance from it. Conversely, covering the shame is about walking alongside in relationship with someone so that restoration might emerge. It is an act of compassion and grace to cover.

> Covering holds the person accountable, but doesn't condemn.
> Covering forgives the failure, and doesn't abandon.
> Covering associates with the outcast, and doesn't discard.
> Covering accepts misperceptions, and doesn't shy away.
> Covering shows hospitality, and doesn't shut the door.
> Covering leads, and doesn't leave behind.
> Covering rebuilds, and doesn't further break.
> Covering hopes, and doesn't lose faith.

We don't always get to choose the risks and risk-takers we lead. Some are mindless, self-serving, negligent, and downright reckless. Will we cover the shame with the hope of redemption and restoration, or will we discard and disassociate as though they are hopeless? How we cover or cover up speaks volumes about our motivations in leading risk, which cannot be covered up.

THE JOURNEY OF RESTORATION

For the rest of our time in Japan, my captain's journey was one of shame and restoration. Not just for him, but for all of us who supported him— his organization, teammates, and friends, and especially his family. In our island fishbowl, many people knew what had happened, and it was a public burden we carried together. My captain may have lost much, but in reclaiming his integrity he restored our respect and bolstered the support of a "covering" community. It was our collective refusal to allow someone's worst moment to be the defining reality of his life. Through it, he experienced redemptive top cover like never before. What started with a confession continued into transformation and led to the recovery of a new servant-leader.

Note: Our "covered" captain has since earned multiple promotions, been a two-time commander, been CFO at the largest installation in Europe, and as I write this, is a senior financial leader serving at the Pentagon. From covered shame to respectable name . . . that's restoration.

LEADING RISK—COVERING THE SPREAD

Is there a reality show better than NCAA basketball's March Madness? I was asked to partner with our Innovation Transformation Office (ITO) to come up with fresh ways to energize ideas and cost savings for the Air Force across the European command. Innovation was the constant buzzword, but as with so many programs under heavy bureaucracy, familiarity only bred contempt. While I appreciated the dedication of my colleagues at the ITO, they were a hodgepodge group of desk pilots, engineers, and analysts stuck deep in the bureaucratic mud.

Our gathering was a painfully long brainstorming session. I was ready to concur with whatever they decided, but the many "rinse and repeat" ideas missed the mark. The general's directive was clear: Grab the attention of the masses, especially the younger generation. As much as I loved tweaks, none of the ITO tweaks would do. So against my better judgment, I chimed in. "I don't think we're meeting the boss's intent." As we were all peers, no one shot me down, but there came the obvious: "So, what's your great idea?" My mind scrambled to where I had been focused earlier in the day—filling out my brackets. Yes, it was that magical time of year when millions of fans and billions of dollars funnel into college basketball's one shining moment, March Madness. I suggested we do a Europe-wide Air Force competition—team against team, base against base, for a collection of the best, most innovative solutions—and call the event Innovation Madness. The ITO hated it, and that convinced me even more. We concluded by agreeing to flesh out our respective ideas, then present to a wider group of stakeholders who would ultimately advise the Four-Star.

I took it back to my team of stellar young officers, those I considered the target demographic, and without hesitation they shouted their approval—another confirmation. Together we fleshed out the details, making sure to keep the competition simple and entertaining. If bases smelled more work and documentation surrounding something they were already doing, the idea would be dead on arrival. Less was truly best.

RISKS ARE BEST COVERED WHEN SHARED

Having risks consistently covered by one person, one team, or one organization is a dangerous place to be. We see this principle illustrated across investments, where a greater variety of assets or an increase in the number of stakeholders helps build leverage while distributing the overall burden. No longer is there a single point of failure, but a portfolio that's been spread with a broader safety net and motivation for gain. Sharing risk alleviates isolated pressures, taps into the depth of diversity, and rewards a greater number when bearing its fruit. This is the same value we find in creating partnerships, working on committees, and collaborating with others. And this was my approach for an innovation program in Europe.

Few things are more unifying and uplifting for a culture than when the risks of a common purpose and goal are spread so that everyone may contribute and cover together (see chapter 3, comparative advantage). In leading risk, we don't do it to individually suffer and then selfishly bask in the glory. We do it so others may be inspired to join hands and, together, do the same—to cover their share and more. Together is where we ideally want to be when it comes to risk reward, and together was where *Innovation Madness* was headed.

—

We presented to the general's advisory staff, and the initial response was overwhelming. They loved the competitive framework and its simplicity. Just like March Madness, we showcased competitive brackets, emphasized social media, and proposed a net-cutting ceremony to *celebrate the champ—no complicated instruction manual and very little paperwork required. The submission of a base's innovative ideas would be captured and summarized through short videos for public consumption. Last, we recommended that $250,000 from the annual budget be the incentive awarded to the winning base. Among the advisory staff, even those who didn't care for March Madness seemed to be energized by the layout and payout. But not ITO. They scrutinized our proposal from beginning to end: "What do you mean, no documentation? What are the milestones and metrics? Who will judge and score the videos? And what will be the scoring mechanism? How will we validate savings?" You could feel the joy and energy being sucked out of the room. "And, there's no way the general's approving $250K without the bases submitting paperwork." It was everything my team had feared— the same conventional, bureaucratic tone that would kill this program on arrival. Those who were on the fence started to retreat toward ITO's conservative, much safer approach. Little to no risk meant little to no chance at failure . . . but it also meant little to no chance at reward. The approach lacked the innovative spirit the program was intended to inspire. How did everyone not see this? Few were willing to cover the spread, their share of the risk, without the security of unanimous support. Risk aversion was up to its antics once again.*

Initially, the majority were excited for a fresh program, but when push came to shove, the staff collectively wavered. ITO was right. We had no baseline of success with this type of competitive approach, and very little had been formalized or tested to ensure further savings would materialize. And yes, $250,000 was arbitrary and perhaps an overly ambitious request for an unproven initial test. We were building the plane as we were flying, embarking on a trial-and-error experiment that intentionally and counterculturally chose not to cross t's and dot i's.

Yet I was firm in my conviction that in order to inspire and unleash innovation among a younger generation of airmen, we needed a measure of reckless abandon and a good dose of competitive fun. As momentum was shifting back to safety, I decided it was time to jump in and cover the spread for those unwilling to do it. ITO, though the lead, refused to be the face presenting this idea to the Four-Star, so I volunteered. I offered to brief the general and if necessary be the fall guy. In

exchange I simply asked for everyone's support at the meeting. After a
brief discussion, the staff and ITO agreed. This was a marginal risk I
was happy to champion.

BE THE CATALYST WHEN NO ONE ELSE WILL

How often have we sat in an audience where everyone has skin in the
game but few people, if any, are willing to challenge the status quo
and suggest the unpopular way forward? Consider the countless great
ideas and golden opportunities that have fallen by the wayside for lack
of simple consensus. Sadly, we know how the story goes. It could have
been so different if there was that one voice, that singular push. We
often find ourselves in a tragic game of "wait and see," where the temptation is to free ride off the courage of others, or as John Stuart Mill
once said, to be "kept (free) by the exertions of better men than ourselves." But risk, like freedom, is a fleeting opportunity. Once it's gone,
it may never return. Who will step up and be that timely, nonconform-
ing voice to take risk and champion the cause when the group is silent?
You will.

But don't worry, what often appears daunting only requires a
tweak. Many are already on board but waiting for that extra measure
of reassurance. Sometimes it's a single vote of confidence that can
make all the difference to convince people to undertake collective risk.
Whatever the need, whether it's being the face or the voice when no
one else will, covering the spread means being ready and willing to
cast that vote. The goal isn't to usurp shared risk, but to decisively encourage it.

—

The time came to brief the Four-Star, and he appeared poker faced
throughout. With reading glasses on, he turned his attention to the de-
tails more than the creative hype. He asked questions similar to ITO's,
but the entire staff stayed connected and prepared for their share of
the risk. We answered that technical and subject-matter experts were
pooled to validate submissions, that the Manpower and Finance offices

were prepared to calculate savings, and that Public Affairs had a plan for the videos and commercials throughout the tournament. Everyone was anxiously awaiting the outcome. When I concluded my presentation, the general removed his reading glasses, looked around the table, and sighed before enthusiastically responding, "Great job, everyone . . . I love it! Let's see if we can carve out five hundred thousand dollars."

—

You would think that in a warrior culture, leading risk would be the norm. But again, the temptation is to stand on the sidelines, especially when the reward has little to no direct, personal bearing. Additionally, the more that careers, promotions, and reputations are at stake, the more risk aversion rules. The majority of us wait to free-ride off the courage of others, when we should be willing to cover the spread and be the difference makers. It doesn't take much to push the consensus forward, but it does take someone.

Note: In its inaugural year, Innovation Madness received over four hundred submissions totaling more than $90 million in reported savings. Nearly a decade later, the program is alive and well, appearing across airwaves in Europe every March. Everyone partook of the risk, everyone celebrated its achievement, and everyone needed someone willing to cover the spread.

CONCLUSION

When's the last time you covered the mess, the shame, or the spread? If you can't recall, then are you leading or managing risk? Imagine if USAA had said, "We're sorry, you're on your own." If they hadn't had my back and the consequences had fallen squarely on me, I'm pretty sure I would have sold the car, moved back on base, and either walked or taxied everywhere. There's no way I would have continued motoring around a city with ten million people. How sad and limited my year in Korea would have been. Instead I continued to drive and explore. Isn't this what we want—the continued spirit of innovation, exploration, and adventure? Don't we desire to see the courage to continually step out in truth, transparency, and integrity? Risk is the only currency that can buy unimaginable rewards. Yet risk may be our most underutilized weapon in leadership because it requires a shift from managing to leading, from fearing to daring, and from an aversion to an embrace. Risk is an enduring commitment, possibly fraught with shame and mess. No wonder, personally and professionally, we've grown comfortable with the self-preserving merits of "managing" risk rather than leading it. Demanded but not exemplified, risk has become a source of hypocrisy. To overcome obstacles in a world filled with constraints, taking risk is our finest weapon. But it takes those who will use the weapon—to lead risk and to cover it.

CHAPTER 9

THE MULTIPLIER EFFECT— INJECTING WELL

I alone cannot change the world, but I can cast a stone across the water to create many ripples.

—Mother Teresa

BLUF: As the writer of Ecclesiastes warns, "Vanity of vanities. . . . All is vanity." How tragic for leaders to start and end without a trace. And how often this happens. We may be here today and gone tomorrow, but a leader's influence was meant to last. For this purpose, leadership is the ultimate platform, unbound by space and time. If we desire the biggest bang for our leadership buck, we must rely on what's known as the multiplier effect—injecting well for lasting ripples.

—

"Dad, what about my opportunity cost?" says the teenager. "Honey, just hire someone—it's not your comparative advantage," says my wife. "No one's listening to your total feedback," says the child being disciplined. "Leave Dad alone. He's stuck in the sunk," says everyone. And if I show any frustration, "He's a negative externality and beyond diminishing returns." There's nothing worse than constantly being challenged and

corrected by your own family. This is the curse of Leadernomics in the home. At the same time, what a blessing to know that what's been injected is being understood, regurgitated, and respent, again and again. Just wish it weren't always being spent on me.

THE MULTIPLIER

Over my years of public speaking, there's nothing better than when a person comes and tells me about the impact Leadernomics has made on their lives, their family, their organization—and yet they've never attended a presentation. Instead they say, "A colleague did, and they told me all about it." Through others, an outer ripple heard the principles and resonated with the stories. This is the power of the multiplier effect. It's when something that's been injected gets reinjected until the cumulative impact is exponential. There's no guarantee of spending or responding, but there's no limit to it either. As with money circulating in the economy, we may not be able to control the behavior of others and their spending patterns, but we can control ours. If the goal is to multiply impact across society, then the injection must be more than just arbitrary and capricious. It requires intentionality. To stimulate the leadership economy we must inject well, and that means injecting readily, strategically, and deeply. By doing so, we tap into the unexpected, the center, and the root value of influence, generating the greatest bang for our leadership buck.

INJECT READILY—THE UNEXPECTED VALUE OF INFLUENCE

While I was a student at the Air Force Academy, I had the opportunity to "Live, Learn, and Intern" in Washington, DC. The program was held at Georgetown University and led by The Fund for American Studies, an educational nonprofit promoting the ideals of freedom to the next generation. To commemorate its twenty-fifth anniversary, the fund hosted a black-tie gala at the Library of Congress and asked if I would introduce the keynote speaker, General Colin Powell. Are you kidding me? *General Powell had just retired from the military after thirty-five years of service, culminating as chairman of the Joint Chiefs of Staff. His autobiography,* My American Journey, *was a New York Times bestseller, and he was rumored to be a leading candidate for the 1996 presidential election. "Of course I'll do it!" When the invitation came, two years had already passed since I graduated from the Academy, and my military service had fallen far short of expectations. I'd found myself trapped in a maze of thirty thousand cubicles, with no airmen to lead and no specialized expertise to offer. So, I volunteered—from charity campaigns to blood drives to intramural sports, even stepping up to lead the most demanding and sensitive office operation, our robust snack bar. As I departed for this trip to DC, my aspirations for leadership and military significance had all but disappeared.*

The Great Hall of the Jefferson Building was adorned in the Italian Renaissance style, with grand murals and vaulted marble ceilings. Tables draped in white linen featuring floral centerpieces and formal place settings filled the room. It was a glorious scene. I grew more nervous by the minute as the list of who's who in politics and business began to enter. Just relax, *I told myself.* Deliver the intro, then quietly disappear. *I went outside to await the general's arrival—and to breathe. Pacing back and forth, I recited aloud the questions I had memorized.* Slap thousand, two thousand. *But as the limo pulled up, everything went blank. The driver opened the door and I began to tumble. Appearing before me, larger than life, was the four-star general and Gulf War hero, the face of CNN and C-SPAN, and quite possibly America's next president. The lowest standing next to the highest; the snack-O walking in with the guest of honor.* What am I doing here? *With sweat beading down my face, I popped the general a salute. Saluting back, he asked, "How are you doing, Lieutenant?"* Terrible. *He sensed it. He placed his hand on my shoulder as if to say everything would be OK. My shirt was drenched, but suddenly, amazingly, the unbearable weight lifted. "Lieutenant, we're going to have a great evening. Now tell me about yourself." And so I did. I told him how nervous I was to meet him . . . that I'd grown up in Chicago . . . that my parents sacrificed everything to emigrate from Korea . . . and that life in the Air Force wasn't turning out how I had expected. The dinner bells had chimed by the time I realized he was the one "escorting" me and not the other way around. Giving the introduction was more than a thrill. It now felt personal. In preparation, I'd come across a story where General Powell's son, then a young Army officer, was set to deploy overseas. He described how his father came to bid him farewell, but didn't offer concerns over his personal safety. Rather, he said, "My dad leaned over, kissed me on the cheek, and gently whispered, 'Take care of our soldiers.'" His focus on others didn't in any way diminish his fatherly love, but only accentuated their common bond and shared calling to lead selflessly and sacrificially.*

As I closed and scurried to the back, General Powell took center stage to a long standing ovation. He opened by answering a question asked earlier in the evening: "Now that you're retired, what do you miss most about being in uniform?" He looked straight in my direction and said, "I miss spending time with the young men and women serving our nation, like Lieutenant Paik." The spotlight shifted, and for the rest of the evening, this nobody became somebody in the eyes of everybody. Before departing, the general gave me a direct order. "Lieutenant, when you get back, find an assignment where you can lead airmen—and don't ever stop leading." If he only knew how this simple injection forever changed my course. "Yes, sir!"

ALWAYS BE PREPARED TO INJECT

I suppose there are countless attributes I could mention about General Powell and the positive spillovers from that evening, but regarding the multiplier, a leader's influence is always prepared to inject. The challenge isn't in the how, but in the now. Do we have the right posture, a willingness to drop dimes of influence whenever and wherever the opportunities arise? A ready posture trusts the power of marginal injections and values the multiplier's unexpected potential. In other words, simplicity doesn't negate magnitude. In fact, one's position and stature are often inversely related to the level of effort required. There's no person or audience too small, no request too difficult, and no agenda so busy that influence is inconvenienced, perceived as irrelevant, and/or aims to withdraw. Being prepared means acknowledging the fleeting nature of each opportune moment and therefore casting a wide net before it disappears.

General Powell could have easily taken a path to dismiss, ignore, and avoid. There were plenty of celebrities and conversations to pull his focus elsewhere. To be protective over his time and interactions would have been perfectly understandable and expected. But he was postured to take a different route. He offered his presence, gave his attention, and used his platform to make me known. He asked, listened, and injected words of wisdom. It didn't need to be lengthy to make a lasting impression. A simple yet timely encounter was all that was needed to jump-start a multiplying effect. We never know when and where we will encounter that captive audience—needing, watching, listening, and waiting. Therefore, the directive to always be prepared is not meant to overwhelm, but to give our injection the best chance of hitting the right people at the right time so that multiplication can readily occur.

INJECT STRATEGICALLY—THE CENTER VALUE OF INFLUENCE

It was as if the general already knew. Just months after the gala, I was selected for reassignment from the land of cubicles to the land of spy planes, Beale Air Force Base, California. From snack-O to leader of thirty airmen, the change was sudden and drastic. Most were only a few years older than me, but light-years ahead in expertise. I depended on their insight, yet they awaited my guidance. I sought their experience, yet they followed my directions. I relied on their performance, yet they were under my evaluation and care. Who was I to hold them accountable, when the trajectory of my career was in the palm of their hands? It all felt backward. It was leadership by fire and a lesson in pure humility.

Every few years, bases would undergo a top-to-bottom inspection to assess mission preparedness. Inspectors were meticulous and antagonistic in their roles, with final reports often making or breaking individual careers. A year after my arrival, it was Beale's turn. I would face my first Air Force Operational Readiness Inspection. I wasn't ready, but my team was. Eight of our best were selected to represent an integrated finance/contracting team. All were E-5s, the rank of an enlisted staff sergeant, and as the sole officer, I was the default team lead. The week-long event tested our teamwork, competency, and stamina. We completed hundreds of different scenarios, many of which were designed to overwhelm and exploit our weaknesses. I had the one foolproof role. As designated spokesperson, all I had to do was accurately voice the answers prepared by my staff sergeants, as they executed their comparative advantage to perfection—providing fast, expert research behind the scenes. Midweek, the inspectors threw us a curveball, "killing" me off to see how the others would respond. Little did they realize my E-5s had all the answers and I was just their talking head. They killed the weakest link—and to their dismay, we finished even stronger. When all was said and done, we were recognized as one of Beale's Outstanding Teams, and as their leader, I was awarded "Superior Performer." Sometimes you gotta take the good and run with it. This single accolade propelled my career for years to come, all because of an outstanding group of staff sergeants, the E-5s.

—

I didn't realize it at the time, but the E-5 represented the largest rank category in the United States Air Force, singlehandedly outnumbering the entire officer corps by five thousand. Though junior officers may have been superior in rank and authority, the E-5s were head and shoulders above in expertise and experience. Similar in age and cultural relevance, we were peers in social circles. We hung out at the same places, listened to similar music, dressed in identical styles, and laughed at the same jokes. On and off duty, we were constantly in each other's line of sight, where the behavior and professionalism of the other was inescapable. There was nothing more piercing than being amid peers who were subordinates, but consistently superior in our profession. Consequently, their mere presence raised the bar for us young officers. And if we didn't elevate our game, we would quickly lose the respect of these peers. The E-5s' influence among junior officers was undeniable, and junior officers comprised more than half the officer corps.

On the enlisted front, E-5s stood at the center-crux. They comprised nearly 27 percent of the enlisted force; directly supervised more than 45 percent (E-1 to E-4); and either miserably or wonderfully impacted the lives of the 19 percent immediately above (E-6). In other words, more than 90 percent of the enlisted force was intimately tied to their daily sphere of influence. If E-5s ever banded together and decided to go on strike, the entire Air Force would be screwed! Corporately, no rank had more top-down, bottom-up, and side-to-side impact than the E-5. The numbers didn't lie. The multiplier effect of the E-5 carried a magnitude far beyond mine alone as a young officer at Beale. Show me a young officer who's surrounded by a group of outstanding, dedicated, professional E-5s, and I'll show you a future commander who will love and appreciate the enlisted force.

CENTER VALUE DISCUSSED, NOT NECESSARILY DEFINED

Simply put, center value is the individual(s) and/or group(s) in our respective organizations and social spheres that carry the greatest potential for proximate and far-reaching impact. This chapter is about getting the biggest multiplying bang for our leadership buck. And so we desire to assess at every level (societal, institutional, organizational, team structure), and in every season, the wisest space, place, and face in which to inject our dimes of influence. In this section I interchangeably use the terms *center target, center value, center mass,* and *center of gravity,* but they're all intended to reflect the same concept: where and with whom our investment will have the greatest impact (sorry, physicists).

Center value isn't always so clear, and there are no hard-and-fast rules for what defines it. Sometimes it is about numbers, and sometimes it's about strength of influence. Sometimes it's the largest group, and other times it may be a single individual. There may be several centers, or there may be a void altogether. It may not necessarily belong to the movers and shakers we think, but to the ones with whom movers and shakers try to ally. Focusing on demographics, percentages, majorities, and size isn't a bad idea, but it may only guide us to the largest target and not the center target. And unless we focus on the center, the outflow from our injection may end up being unilateral rather than multidimensional.

We should objectively consider facts, but we must also subjectively engage and look closer, trying to almost experience where the center may be. Who are the informal leaders? Where do people go for proficiency and expertise? Where do people gravitate for decisions and advice? To whom do people adhere, defer, and always show respect? Does the center influence lie within positions, or perhaps popularity? We're not searching for a needle in a haystack, but looking to hit that big ole sweet spot where the outward impact of our influence gets paid forward in all directions.

As crude as this may sound, we only have so many pearls to give, so don't give your pearls to swine. We want our pearls to go where they'll be prized. With your pearls of experience, hard knocks, wisdom, and insight, whom will you mentor? Who would most prize them? Or better yet, if you were to send an open invitation, who would come and be in your audience? And who would you want in your audience?

Because of their early impact on me personally and professionally, and then later throughout my career, the E-5 always held a special place in my "center value" heart. I know general officers are politically and strategically influential—they're ones who decide the course of our respective armed services, and the faces we see in the media making wartime history—but not once in my career did I hear anyone at any level, home or deployed, or among any of our sister services (Army, Navy, and Marines), say, "I sure could use another general (or admiral)." If practical necessity is the driving factor behind center value, then sorry, generals . . . you're not it. If daily, face-to-face, in-person influence across the masses is the deciding factor, again, generals, you're not it. And if it's about the productivity, workload, and gross numbers impacted by your supervision, then, generals, you're definitely not it.

But throughout my career, wherever I've gone, I've repeatedly heard "How can I get more E-5s?" And the context has always centered around the most important matter: accomplishing the mission. The plea is always for more junior leaders who can supervise, train, and conduct their primary trade with matchless performance and productivity. Mission execution and compliance with standards depend on the backbone of these young leaders and doers. And so I ask, "Who could use a few more E-5s?" Add to this the reality of their numbers, their demographics, and their strategic positioning among the ranks, and though I'm not 100 percent certain they're *the* center of gravity, I wouldn't bet against it. Is the daily level of support, attention, investment, and development that we pour into the E-5 commensurate with their collective importance? I didn't think so. So I decided to do my part. After all, I did owe them for a few promotions in my career.

—

As I peeled back the layers, the data was clear. If the E-5 is below average, then the United States Air Force is destined to be below average. But if the E-5 is incredible, like my group was at Beale, then we would continue to be the greatest Air Force the world has ever known. To positively influence this single category would produce an externality of unmatched strategic importance.

Airman Leadership School (ALS) needed to be my go-to venue. Each class held a captive audience of rising E-5s. But gaining access to their stage wasn't easy, especially as I was a young officer. The curriculum was tightly controlled by senior enlisted leaders—what I called the "Chiefs Mafia." And rightfully so. ALS was the United States Air Force's final rite of passage to gaining the keys to supervision. But I took General Powell's directive to heart and wouldn't stop trying. In a somewhat condescending manner, a Chief would suspiciously inquire, "Sir, what's the message you want to give?"

I would earnestly respond, "To show E-5s the mirror, that they might see who they are—personally, organizationally, and corporately." The word *corporately would always provoke just enough curiosity to get me the invite. For the next twenty-plus years, I spoke to every ALS class I could get my hands on. It became my favorite speaking engagement and one of my greatest privileges while serving our nation. If someone asked me, "Now that you're retired, what do you miss most?" I would say, "Spending an afternoon with a group of E-5s."*

AGGRESSIVELY INVEST IN CENTER CAPITAL

If and when we recognize an opportunity with center value, it's time to knock down doors, gather them in, give discounts, send coupons, whatever it takes to fill our leadership theater. Inject and invest liberally. No waiting around. Go! Center value is the group we must intentionally and proactively pursue. We must place a premium on their human-capital investment, training and education, and leadership enhancement. And with planning and purpose, we must engage and mentor to carve a long-term path for them to follow. If center mass is within the mid to lower ranks, few will possess the boldness to ask for injections, so engage with them and cast the net widely. Our leadership capacity is greater than we realize. Give pearls to center mass if you want to hit critical mass in multiplication.

INJECT DEEPLY—THE ROOT VALUE OF INFLUENCE

Having moved fifteen times to include six countries in twenty-five years, I often had the "get in and get out" mindset: Do your job and leave. If I had it my way, we wouldn't have unpacked the majority of our boxes or put up so many pictures—less work for the next move. I never craved an extended community or felt burdened by not having one. As long as I had my family, I was good. I preferred quietness and privacy. Besides, why go through the struggles and emotions of investing in new relationships again and again—neighbors, churches, friends—only to uproot shortly thereafter? And it wouldn't be fair to those who reciprocate. Better to just skim the surface and go rather than leaving them hanging. But my wife would have none of that. Community had always been her lifeblood, and diving heart-first to cultivate even the slightest bit of depth was her ever-present mission. It wasn't up for debate. Her directive to the family was always "Get in and get deep, no matter our duration." She believes that character development, fulfillment, and growth always happen faster and deeper in the context of community. This explains her throwing birthday surprises in Korea and hosting weekly luncheons with all the ladies. It's why she organized baby showers and housewarming parties for colleagues and neighbors in Colorado, and the reason we invited all my classmates in Alabama for a Chicago-style Super Bowl. We deep-fried turkeys for Friendsgiving in Louisiana and hosted oyster roasts and crawfish boils in South Carolina. In Okinawa, Japanese children and their parents filled our tiny home, dressed in costumes, ready to trick-or-treat. And in Germany, our home became a central hub among the many villages for Bible studies and small-group gatherings. Whether it was a three-year marathon or a ten-month sprint, stateside or overseas, it didn't matter. My wife made sure we were building relationships and digging deep. And over time, it multiplied our community globally, in ways we could have never imagined.

BE PLANTED TO INJECT MUTUALLY

If any family has reason to keep their connections shallow, it's the military family. Since we were always on the move, it seemed sensible to stay on the surface and keep a healthy distance—not getting too close, too involved, or overly invested. But failing to root where planted also meant superficial relationships, limited growth, and minimal mutual injection. And my wife knew it.

Creating depth wasn't easy, but it was reciprocated tenfold without reservation or regret. It was a blessing to give, but we were constantly being outdone in return. Before deploying to Iraq, I wondered how my wife would survive the year alone in a new community with three toddlers in tow. But she quickly made a community of friends and neighbors who made sure there was always help on the scene.

Friends replaced tires and changed the oil, and contributed toward carpools, babysitting, and assistance with meals. And during a hurricane alert, neighbors came and tied down loose boards, secured windows, and brought our patio furniture into the garage. She ended up never being alone, and in fact she made her closest friendships while I was away. Depth's reciprocation provided her a network of support that not only sustained her, but enabled our kids to thrive. Their well-being was my peace of mind, and not once during my mission was my focus compromised. If we wonder how our military is able to repeatedly deploy, do their mission, and constantly thrive, anytime anywhere, look no further than the spouse's support network. When planted deep, it's the ultimate force multiplier.

BE PLANTED TO INJECT THAT WHICH MATTERS MOST

Depth meant tireless hospitality—preparing, hosting, cooking, and cleaning. It meant selflessly serving—caring for another's pet, home, or children. It meant sympathizing and empathizing—listening, sharing, and embracing. It meant being open—willing to appreciate different cultures, faiths, and opinions. And it meant doing life with others in transparency and vulnerability. *Depth injected life into life. It's here that influence transcends formality and bears an unmistakable authenticity.* In taking root, we were introduced to families, customs, and cultures that forever changed our perspective. We experienced friendships where our hardships were carried together, and we were allowed access into the sacred parts of others' lives, the places where hopes, fears, and anxieties reside. The quality and intensity of depth exceeded the depth that comes from duration. Despite having no assignment longer than three years, we were welcomed into others families' greatest joys and darkest moments.

We journeyed promotions, birthdays, weddings, and pregnancies, just as we journeyed marital conflicts, divorces, terminal illnesses, and death. Depth, more than duration, was the price of walking the journey together, and in the process, speaking into the lives of others. Taking root gave us exclusive access into hearts and minds for our deepest injections: faith, hope, and love; values, beliefs, and ideals; character, vision, and passion. In the end, isn't this what we desire to leave behind? Isn't this the lasting legacy we yearn to multiply? Rooted relationships paved the way to softer hearts and kindred spirits to form a lifelong bond. That which matters most takes more than ready words and strategic actions. It takes being planted in relationship. When we inject deeply, we realize the root value isn't always about numbers, but about a quality that lasts, mutual enrichment that satisfies the soul, and a lifetime of joys untold. This is where the multiplier bears its greatest fruit.

BE PLANTED TO INJECT INTO HUMANITY

It's easy to inject into people who are similar to us and/or demonstrate a desire to be multiplied. They're talented, ambitious, teachable, humble, and passionate. We would all love such protégés. But what about those who are considered different, less fortunate, awkward, unqualified? What about society's marginalized? Who will abundantly inject into those who don't have the ability to pay it forward—the poor, the sick, the homeless, the elderly, those on their deathbed? Who will reach out and be that support network for the least of these? And it doesn't stop there. How do we see those whom society deems unqualified as leaders due to subjective biases like race, class, gender, age, or any of the biases that false narratives use to determine worth? Who will mentor across these subjective biases? When we inject into humanity, we're injecting into the dignity and significance of every person regardless of biases, including our own and those that others may have about us.

—

While we were stationed in Germany in 2016, my wife developed a friendship with our daughter's French tutor. He was an older gentleman who had moved from France much later in life. We never learned his full story, but we knew there was a divorce and unreconciled brokenness in his family's past. He had a new life in Germany but would often dwell on the sadness of being abandoned by his children and left alone. My wife developed a good friendship, always having conversations with him after lessons, and seeking to learn a few phrases herself. After he missed several sessions with our daughter, we inquired and learned that he had been hospitalized with cancer. It was terminal, and his decline was rapid. Without community and without hope, his final months would have been spent in a sterile hospital, alone, but my wife remained by his side till the end and inspired the rest of us to join her. When he passed, she helped organize the funeral. No family members came. It was just our family and our pastor. Our time with him was simply a priceless investment in humanity. There's no greater multiplier within the human spirit than to experience the depths of human compassion, especially when it's focused on those who can't pay it forward. Injecting into humanity is injecting into the deepest part of oneself, where multiplication has no bounds.

CONCLUSION

We were in Hawaii snorkeling when I realized . . . my wife's a fish. I couldn't get her out of the water. While I remained content on the surface, she would dive as far and as deep as possible. I didn't understand the effort. With such clear waters I could see plenty of colorful fish and bright coral to keep me entertained. I imagined that what she saw farther beneath the surface was only marginally different. Why go through the effort of diving deeper? When she finally surfaced, the look in her eyes said it all. Something magical had occurred. The images, the feelings, the experience . . . the depth of her rich description dwarfed mine in seconds, revealing an appreciation far beyond what I would ever know. A multiplying impact had taken place and kept reinjecting for more. We may have been in the same waters, but we spent our afternoon in two different worlds.

—

How readily, strategically, and deeply are you injecting? Is your influence keeping near the shore or daring to make ripples?

—

I once asked a group of young officers during a mentor session if influencing and inspiring others was a part of their vocational calling. To my surprise, the unanimous response was no. Nice but optional. If it happens, it happens. To claim leadership without a vision to multi-ply future leaders is surface leadership at best. We can be visionaries, entrepreneurs, great managers and performers without ever experiencing the depths of multiplying leadership. To inject readily and strategically is a great start, but it can't end there if we want to experience the riches of that different world. To enrich souls and speak into parts unknown, to multiply leaders for generations to come, we must take root and plant deep. As my wife would say, "Once you go deep, you'll never wish to stay on the surface."

CHAPTER 10

POSITIVE AND NORMATIVE ECONOMICS—THE FINAL TEST

School is not . . . learning to live but [is] obliged to be
life itself. For you must learn from life . . . not about it.
—John Hersey, author of *Hiroshima*

BLUF: Our transformative journey is to be lived, not merely studied
or hypothetically considered. As we experience firsthand the ups and
downs, the joys and failures, the mysteries and self-discoveries, there's
a tension along the way. Between present reality and a future vision,
being and becoming, and the here and now versus the not yet seen, the
concern is that we tend to veer to one side. But positive and normative
economics constantly set us toward a more holistic path. From objective demands ("what *is*") to subjective insights ("what *should* be"), the
tension is meant to both tug and to guide, revealing where we are and
reminding us where we ought to be.

—

The morning of 9/11 began like any other Colorado morning—me running late for class and my wife taking care of our newborn. But as I scurried past, her eyes were glued to the news. "Seung," she said, "a plane just crashed into the World Trade Center." Outside the north entrance of the Air Force Academy, an unusually long line had formed. I dialed my department when a colleague informed me of another crash . . . a second plane. By the time I arrived, the world had changed. The typically lighthearted buzz of college students turned gravely sober. Many were in tears and asked to be excused. The rest sat silent, stunned, contemplative. What would this mean going forward? I didn't realize it at that moment, but this was our Pearl Harbor, and I was no longer just their econ teacher. How would we navigate these next steps? Where would economics take us from here? Where should it take us?

—

My introductory class followed the standard text, beginning with positive economics. The definitions and models explained the behaviors and outcomes as seen in a market economy. Supply and demand led the way, with pricing and incentives close behind. Positive economics observed and described "what is," explaining cause-and-effect relationships that were objective and provable. Steering clear of opinions and value judgments, there was nothing sacred, vulnerable, or personal about it—just a matter-of-fact study. But in the days following 9/11, our progression in the positive lost all momentum. Supply-and-demand models garnered zero interest, and age-old examples seemed to bear little connection to life's sudden imperatives. The tragic loss of three thousand lives compelled a more introspective journey, and unless a meaning-filled dialogue could ensue, my lectures would quickly fade toward irrelevance. Did the "positive" possess a conscience? My students demanded to know. They yearned for something deeper—to engage in a discussion of "what should be," not to hear another lecture describing "what is." So, skipping ahead, I introduced positive's passionate, idealistic twin.

THE NORMATIVE DIFFERENCE: "WHAT SHOULD BE"

While positive economics centers on analytical imperatives, normative economics weighs social and ethical implications. The former observes and explains market behavior, while the latter seeks to advise it. In 1999, someone put a human kidney up for auction on eBay. The starting bid of $25,000 skyrocketed toward $6 million. If there's a market of many buyers but only one seller for a highly desirable yet rare commodity, positive analysis will demonstrate the market's ability to take price on a wild ride. Unemotional and systematic, positive objectively unfolds "what is." The normative, on the other hand, steps back and asks, Should human organs be sold and purchased in the open market at all? Regardless of the number of willing buyers and sellers and their mutual consent for gain, normative is mindful of the immediate and long-term effects such transactions may have across society. Far more than the proper workings of supply and demand and the accuracy of data-driven models, normative is concerned with equity and fairness, justice and order, values and ideals that are either being carefully advanced or dangerously violated. Normative doesn't dismiss the positive but is informed by it, discerning and cautious for the sake of moral convictions and social welfare. It understands the human condition and our proclivity toward incentives. Therefore, normative targets policy decisions. It isn't passive, indifferent, or apathetic, but opinionated and assertive. It's the normative where emotions get engaged, fiery debates are entered, and the battle for society is tirelessly fought.

An open market for human organs would likely exploit the poor and the desperate. The eBay auction presented a steep and slippery slope toward the commodification of humans, exacerbating the harsh realities of abuse, objectification, and manipulation. The enormous dollar amounts at stake would likely incentivize perverse and criminal behavior. And without market intervention, issues of safety, sanitation, and fraud were sure to arise—externalities carrying deadly consequences. Inhumane harm has no limits when self-interest is left completely unguarded. Normative isn't blind to this evil and therefore anticipates irrational and immoral behavior, market failures, and anything else that might corrupt the standard models and assumptions. It's through normative analysis that policies and social norms for human organs have evolved. Never again has a platform like eBay conducted such an auction, and the consequences for illegal transactions are quite severe. Not only has the normative led to a national database and network of donors, but it has refined the criteria by which recipients are prioritized in accordance with medical concerns and moral values rather than persuaded by socioeconomic disparities or political whims. Public campaigns have helped to spread awareness, to inform and educate, and to spur an exponential growth in the number of donors. And greater transparency has led to a safer, more dignified allocation of donated organs. It's the normative that has led to a more humane, equitable, and robust "market" of care, where even the marginalized "consumer" can have hope. This is "what should be" impacting "what is."

—

Our semester's watershed moment came when a student asked, "Sir, should human life be priced?" It was a normative question, but what provoked it? The student then referenced a news article regarding a special provision for victims of 9/11. Congress had approved a compensation fund totaling $7 billion. The money would be used to financially assist family members of the deceased and those who were injured. But to file, claimants would need to waive their rights to any future civil case against the airlines, thus protecting the industry from thousands of potential lawsuits and possible insolvency. In the classroom, positive and normative shots were fired: Who decided $7 billion? Why only $250,000 for pain and suffering? Can any amount adequately capture their true loss? What will be their methodology? And will some receive more than others? Do the airlines deserve protection from insolvency? Pandora's box was shattered. In the eyes of my students, no objective calculation could satisfy the chasm between "what is" and "what should be." It seemed irreconcilable. Amid rising frustrations, I interrupted. "So are we suggesting the fund be dissolved and every victim be left to their own?" If Congress were to decide that the fund should be more, *how much more would be appropriate? Should it be $20 billion, $100 billion, $1 trillion? Is there a "right" amount? For the injured, should the compensation for pain and suffering be undefined and unlimited? And if so, who will foot the bill? Should we allow the airlines to go bankrupt? How might their collapse affect our commerce, our security, our nation? I even went so far as to ask, "Are insurance companies and their data scientists corrupt and evil, and should their voice to policymakers be silenced?" The class ended in a stalemate, and it was perfect.*

THE POSITIVE-NORMATIVE TENSION: GOOD OR BAD? FACT OR MYTH?

If someone came to your door and issued you a check for a lost loved one in the amount of X, how many of you would say, "Thank you, that seems about right"? As with the auction for a human organ, the tension centered on "what is" versus "what should be." No dollar amount could speak to intrinsic worth or recover priceless loss, and to suggest an actuarial payout felt coldhearted. No matter how well intended, it was sure to offend. But no one dared to dissolve the fund. They understood that for those in financial straits, something was still better than nothing, and it went a long way in alleviating such burdens. At the same time, none of my students attempted to advocate for a limitless provision or an undefined payout. This too was unaffordably offensive. The conviction of infinite value was once again being confronted by the reality of scarcity. Life was indeed priceless, and no amount of resources could fully satisfy its loss. It was the normative wrestling with the positive, and neither could pin the other.

But this wasn't "bad." In fact, what would have been concerning is if there was no tension at all. The gap between "what is" and "what should be" wasn't a moral failure, but a fact of life. The tension was actually a loudspeaker for good, if properly heard and understood. The failure wasn't in the calculations but in the methodology's strict approach, with arbitrary limits and poor optics. How the normative was given little-to-no voice seemed unacceptable. From the onset, the approach was rudimentary and void of qualitative considerations, limits were ill-explained, the variance in payouts was widely discriminatory, and the message of altruism was distorted by deadlines and nonfiling agreements against the backdrop of lawsuits. For a purpose as significant and sensitive as this, the delivery was calculated, impersonal, and transactional. The program, though intended to do good, openly missed the mark. Several myths were exposed and truths confirmed.

Positive and Normative Economics, Though Distinct, Are Not at Odds

In fact, the two are complementary and were meant to coexist to best serve humanity. The outcomes and behaviors revealed in the positive are used and assessed to guide in the normative. In the case of the 9/11 fund, the response by victims and their public outcry spoke volumes to policymakers. It's what ultimately drove a different normative response. More than just about protecting the airlines, it became a means by which our nation was able to tangibly serve and sincerely sympathize with the enormity of personal loss.

"What is" May Be Factual, Objective, and Descriptive, but It's Also Subject to Change

When the normative is esteemed and handled with care, policies and methodologies can begin to follow. This is what changes "what is." And it's the normative that leads the way. A departure from the fixed, inflexible approach was required, and unlike what happened at the program's onset, priceless voices became welcomed and heard. The impersonal turned personal, the quantitative received qualitative feedback, and exceptions started to be made.

Pricing the Priceless Isn't a Violation of the Normative; the Violation Is to Not Price At All

Sometimes pricelessness results in the "futile effect" where we think nothing can seemingly satisfy, so why bother? If apathy is the alternative, then price, price, price. Though lacking in sentiment, something is still better than nothing when the need is real. Many families faced severe financial hardship as a result of 9/11, and despite any flawed approach or poor optics to the compensation, waiting on "what should be" was something they could ill afford. Dissolving the fund or not making any provisions at all would have been far more egregious. Pricing served as a catalyst to get the normative discussion rolling.

The Normative May Be Idealistic, but It Serves the Greatest Practical Good

With its influence upon laws, policies, and social norms, the normative carries perhaps the greatest practical impact to society. It's the conviction of intrinsic value and priceless worth that ultimately stirs hearts toward action and long-term change.

BREAKING IT DOWN IN LEADERSHIP TERMS

Teaching at a leadership laboratory, I pretty much had carte blanche at the Academy to vector anything and everything toward a leadership discussion. So it was time for the class to learn a critical lesson from baseball. Because of my small size, I only played baseball competitively through middle school, but it didn't take a wealth of experience to know the difference between a fastball and a curveball. If you've got to keep your eyes on one, then there's only one to pick.

The Positive Curveball

The positive, "what is," spells out the matter-of-fact in leadership—the objective, measurable results that are descriptive and provable. It's all the stuff that leaders use to assess teams and individuals, but it's also the stuff by which they themselves are judged. Across different industries and professions, the language may vary, but the intent is the same: Knock "what is" out of the park, or else. For coaches, deliver wins and championships; for CEOs, deliver profits and earnings; for public officials, deliver on promises made; and for military leaders, deliver mission success—strategically, operationally, and tactically. Even the clergy can feel the pressure to deliver growth in the way of members and tithes. And across every field, everyone must deliver more with less. It's never a "one and done" that can be permanently satisfied. But like a curveball, delivering on the positive means hitting a moving and fluctuating target. We must constantly set our eyes on it, or we'll likely miss and look exceedingly bad.

The Normative Fastball

The normative, "what should be," in leadership centers on the stuff of immeasurable, subjective worth and priceless value. It echoes a familiar sentiment: "Take care of your people, and your people will take care of the mission." The fastball is the bread-and-butter pitch that reflects the "why" in leadership—our source of inspiration and motivation. The normative encompasses our vision, core values, ideals, and nonnegotiables, and of course, our people. "What should be" emphasizes a human connection—to preserve, protect, and advance the welfare of society today and tomorrow. The normative is not about self-preservation, our paychecks, promotions, or rewards; rather, it's about our cause and the people we lead in fighting the good fight.

Which Ball Do We Eye?

To succeed, we should be mindful of both the positive curveball and the normative fastball, but it's the curveball that overwhelmingly catches our eye. Show me a leader who fails in the positive, and I'll show you a leader who won't last in the normative. At least that's the threat. Like anything in the marketplace, everyone gets priced. We're ascribed a "what is" valuation as creators, entrepreneurs, producers, workers, entertainers, and leaders. We're inputs to labor, performance, and production, and whether we like it or not, whether it's right or wrong, unless key indicators are met, we won't sustain our value very long. The positive assigns to us a present market value and a future numerical worth that demand our attention. It's the strikeout pitch we seemingly can't afford to miss. You've heard the saying "That which gets measured gets done." The positive gets measured, and therefore we place our focus on getting it done.

But in doing so, we tend to overlook the pitch we grew up with— the most basic of leadership principles. The normative fastball is the one we take for granted because of its familiarity. We think we'll be able to always hit it, but it's the pitch that speeds past when overlooked, leaving us unable to recover. This is what happens when we fixate on the curveball. We consistently miss our bread-and-butter pitch, and it's our quickest way out of the big leagues. The curveball may make us look bad, but to miss the fastball is to lose our people. This is striking out on the heart and soul of our leadership. One can sit on the fastball and still adjust for the slower curve, but not vice versa. If there's to be any hope at hitting both, it must always be with eyes disciplined on the fastball first.

CURVEBALL LEADERSHIP

Our first year of marriage, I had one of those bosses who lived in the positive and had no qualms about it. He would lock his office door to work on his seminar courses required for promotion, while the rest of us were performing the mission. His demands regularly extended into weekends, and it became his habit to call me in on Saturdays for whatever tasks he deemed necessary. As active-duty military, we were 24/7, and so as long as his request wasn't illegal or immoral, my only response would be "Yes, sir."

My new bride had zero familiarity with military life and culture, which made it all the more amazing that she did not once complain. No shots fired at me, my boss, or the Air Force. On one particular weekend, we had made plans to travel to Seoul and spend the day, but instead, once again, I had to break the bad news. I thought for sure this would be the end of her rope. But she offered the same gracious understanding. I clearly married the right one. As my wife got up early to pack me lunch and watch me leave, I put on my uniform and thanked her for being so supportive. Then I heard her say, "It's OK, I know we can use the extra pay." My eyes popped, and my heart dropped. All I could do was creep away. Otherwise my expression would have said it all. This was not the time to clarify. But later that evening, when I confessed that there was no such thing as "overtime" . . . let's just say it was a rough night, and the beginning of a tough first year of marriage. Welcome to the military, honey!

THE SLIPPERY SLOPE TO COMMODIFICATION

It was my first experience working for a person who led behind a curveball. The tyranny of the urgent was always his claim. Yet there wasn't
a single task I can recall that would have been considered mission es-
sential, requiring every weekend. This was the same boss who threatened to fire my young lieutenant because of his poor presentation and
the one who regularly skipped the chain to get whatever, whenever he
needed it. He was all smiles around peers and leaders, but not around
us. What perhaps was on the line was his performance rating entering
another promotion cycle, and the need to show hard results. His focus
on the curveball without an eye for the fastball turned into a slippery
slope toward commodification. We all felt more like inputs to production for his advancement than humans to be considered and cared for.

Commodification may sound like a strong word to use when
describing the people we lead, but we don't get here by mistake. In
leadership, when there's an overemphasis on achieving the positive
(whatever the motive) and a lack of emphasis on esteeming the normative, commodification is the inevitable outcome. It's meant to describe situations where people are viewed and valued more as market
commodities (e.g., human organs, actuarial stats) than as entities with
inherent value. The terminology is based on market transactions more
than human relations—where a person is assessed as an object or a
resource rather than as an individual. The commodifier says, "So long
as our people are performing and producing, they will be viewed as
having worth." But anyone who doesn't measure up is considered less
valuable and, in the extreme, disposable. When we fall prey to positive's incentives but lose sight of "what should be," it's a descent toward
using, abusing, and discarding. Ask yourself some basic questions
about your organization and its leaders:

- How are people greeted and introduced?
- How are people tasked and assigned?
- How are people listened to? Are they given a voice? Do
  they have a name?
- How are people treated when times are tough, or when
  they're injured or sick?

- How are people fired or informed of being let go?
- How are people provided feedback and performance appraisals?
- How are bonuses and promotions handled?
- How about reorganizations and the shuffling of personnel? How are they accomplished?
- How are people moved from one position to the next?
- Are people given a farewell?

In all these questions, there's either a "price" or "priceless" message being conveyed. In sports, you'll often hear players say when they're abruptly traded, "It's just a business." But if you read between the lines, what do you hear? And what does that mean? The thing about commodification is that once it becomes a part of the culture, the habit can easily go in all directions. Both leaders and their people become nothing more than an input to gain a certain output. One piece of evidence may be found in an organization's turnover rate. When people rapidly come and go, it often points to a lack of commitment and loyalty, and a breakdown in relational obligations. I used to think that the temptation toward commodification was greater in larger organizations and institutions, but I've come to realize that it happens across the board. No one is immune from an overly focused curveball, especially when people are looking to quickly advance. Beware of their tendency to commodify everyone around them. The saddest part about commodification if you're a leader is that you may get the results you seek, but you should never expect to get more. That requires the normative.

FASTBALL LEADERSHIP

After my experience in Korea, I was ready to get out of the service. I had completed more than my five years of required active-duty commitment, and I knew I didn't want to work for another boss like the one I had. My wife wouldn't have allowed it.

But then came the opportunity of a lifetime. I was asked to return to my alma mater and teach at the United States Air Force Academy.

It was an offer I couldn't refuse. The application and interview process was fairly rigorous but worthwhile. You never know what the leadership and culture will be like until you're immersed in it, but a good number of professors from when I was a cadet were still on faculty, and I couldn't wait to be a part of the team.

From the moment I arrived, the contrast between my organization in Korea and the Academy exceeded all expectations. I went from curveball commodification to fastball leadership. There were plenty of "what is" demands on all of us, with many additional duties piled onto the load of classes and students. But the primary focus remained on "what should be." Metrics mattered, but the normative mattered more and it fostered a culture that was personal, relational, hospitable, collegial, and family-oriented. After the overbearing micromanagement I had experienced in Korea, I could hardly believe the amount of freedom, trust, and autonomy I was given from day one. The level of formal and informal mentorship I received proved critical for this new instructor, but it wasn't only for me. It was widely offered by all the seasoned professors to all the junior instructors. When I would ask the more senior members in the department about my newfound freedom and autonomy, the response was always consistent, "Oogy," (my nickname in the department), "we hire great people and then get out of their way." All I knew was that I was going to go above and beyond to ensure that statement was true. In those three years of teaching, I worked harder than I did at any previous assignment I had in the Air Force and produced far more "what is" results—including the creation of Leadernomics—than I was ever required or asked to do. It was a normative lesson learned.

If there was any doubt about the power of the normative surrounding this department's leadership, the battle for my next assignment proved it once and for all. The department had selected me for a PhD opportunity, but my career field had other plans. They denied the request and told my department head I couldn't be released for the PhD. When my boss asked what other plans they had, they failed to provide a specific response. He had his reservations, and so he asked me, "If they're not going to release you for a PhD, what would you like to do instead, and where would you and Grace most want to go? We'll make sure that's in 'their plan.'" He wasn't going to allow for a default assignment and decided to personally go to bat for me, for my career and my advancement. He chose to be proactive and deliberate in getting me where I wanted and needed to go. He believed I had earned it and was going to do whatever he could to make that happen. And sure enough, he did.

If my boss in Korea was the epitome of positive, then my department head at the Academy was the face of normative. At every turn, he personalized the impersonal, perceptively changed transactions into relationship decisions, and conveyed to me a message of my priceless worth. Him focusing on "what should be" inspired me to happily give my all toward "what is," and then some. Metrics and the bottom line never seemed to be his primary motive, but it somehow became everyone's willing byproduct. It reminded me that positive and normative are not at odds, but that when the normative is highly esteemed and prioritized, the positive has a chance to be unimaginable. Pricing the priceless is a fact of life, but it wasn't meant to replace the normative. Leaders, we are to close the gap between the two. The normative serves more than just an idealistic purpose; it ultimately produces the greatest positive results. Reconciling the immeasurable distance between the positive and the normative, "what is" and "what should be," requires priceless leaders to care for their priceless people through their priceless acts.

CLOSING THE GAP—THE LEADER'S INTERVENTION

Tension between the positive and the normative is not meant to confuse, but is rather an opportunity for leaders to defuse by reconciling the difference. What if our actions to promote the positive could always carry a normative message/agenda? Consider what difference the following approach would make:

- delegating tasks . . . to train, teach, and empower our people
- assigning responsibilities . . . to elevate and broaden their level of experience

- striving after growth . . . to expand roles and opportunities for others
- maximizing profits . . . to be generously shared with those who earned them
- prioritizing savings . . . to reinvest in human capital and professional development
- achieving goals . . . to support our people's referrals and recommendations
- pursuing championships . . . to cement their legacy and reward their greatest efforts
- reducing costs . . . to protect and preserve the most jobs
- meeting hard deadlines . . . to secure bonuses and time off for our people
- accomplishing metrics . . . to highlight and recognize their excellence
- elevating expectations . . . to professionally stretch and personally challenge
- building networks . . . to launch rising leaders and extend to them opportunities elsewhere

The priceless leader is mindful to actively engage in closing the positive/normative gap. More than just about achieving the bottom line, it's about using the bottom line for others. More than about protecting and advancing the leader's personal pursuits, the positive becomes a means to preserve, protect, and advance the organization for the sake of our people's pursuits. It's about utilizing everything at our disposal as leaders so that we may reinvest it back into those who made it happen. In other words, "what is" is never good enough unless it serves "what should be."

When the positive has the power to inform, serve, esteem, and elevate the normative, striving after metrics can be done selflessly and wholeheartedly with joy. And when your people can see that price is used to serve the priceless and not the other way around (i.e., commodification), they will often stay, contribute, excel, commit, remain loyal, and give it their all even though they could earn more pay elsewhere. This is a leader who doesn't just get it, they "gap" it. And it makes all the difference.

CONCLUSION

Which way are we veering?

—

As I wrapped up my master's thesis at Penn State University, the final months became a race to the finish. I was on a one-year scholarship and needed to complete the program before reporting for duty in Ohio. Falling further and further behind schedule, I found myself buried and isolated in the computer lab, neglecting both self-care and buddy-care. The friends I had made in my men's group were persistent in reaching out, but I had no time for them. It was crunch time and not relationship time. One night after returning from the lab, I found one of those friends, a mentor, sitting at my apartment door with a glorious pizza in hand. "Have time for a bite?" I hadn't seen him in weeks, and I felt terrible for not returning his calls. But he acted as if all was well, and that put me at ease. We scarfed down the pizza and had a few laughs. Then we shared a conversation that was brief, but perhaps one of the most unforgettable ones I've ever had. He started innocently enough: "Oogy, you must really love this econ stuff?"

Me: Yeah, I do.

Friend: So you must know a lot about investing?

Me: Sure, the basic principles. Like diversification, time value of money, dollar cost averaging. Enough to get started.

Friend: That's great. So let me ask you a question. Do you believe there's anything that's eternal?

Me: (Hmm, where was he going with this?) Uh, yeah . . . God and people.

Friend: So what do you think about investing your time, talents, and resources for eternal returns? Is that a good econ decision?

I loved his approach, and his message was profound. In that moment, in all my busyness, buriedness, self-centeredness, and buddy-carelessness, he closed the gap toward the normative and reminded me that I was missing out on something far more valuable. I may have been investing deeply in achieving positive returns (i.e., my studies, my degree, my advancement), but in the process, I was neglecting the

surrounding normative: investing in friendships bearing eternal re-
turns. It was a timely word and a simple yet priceless act. He concluded
by saying, "We all miss you and hope you'll spend time with us before
you leave for Ohio." And I did.

—

As we'd say at the margin, if you're going to keep your eye on only one ball, make sure it's the right one. Don't miss any opportunities to convey to those you lead that they are of priceless value. That's the greatest economic investment you can make. Show me a leader who strives to close the gap between "what is" and "what should be," and I'll show you followers who will strive to live up to their priceless value. In the marketplace, we're paid for the value we add, not for our inherent value. My friend, who knew no econ, reminded me of the greatest economic investment—one made with inherent value in mind. That's leadership. We get the treasured platform of leading people of priceless value and eternal worth. Leadership and economics have always been *human* endeavors to defeat commodification and hold in highest regard our greatest inputs to production, our people. May you inject well, may you lead well, and may you invest deeply in that which has eternal returns.

PRICE VERSUS VALUE— OUR DAILY BATTLE

> Price is what you pay; value is what you get.
> —Warren Buffett

I had just returned from Iraq, and the timing couldn't have been better. Our tenth wedding anniversary was right around the corner, and friends living in Germany had invited us to join them on a European vacation. I had never been, and my wife was dying to go. But it wouldn't be easy. Traveling across the Atlantic with three kids and an armful of suitcases was hardly romantic. We hopped on a space-available C-17 from Charleston, South Carolina, to Ramstein, Germany, with earplugs, our luggage on pallets, and Humvees next to our feet. But midflight it became a memorable family camping trip as we sprawled across the open floor in sleeping bags.

Upon arrival, it was straight to the local Hofbräu for the best soft pretzels, German beer, and schnitzel. As the evening was about to conclude, our friends presented an anniversary surprise. On the table, they placed car keys and a map with Paris circled. "We'll take care of the kids," they said. "Go enjoy your tenth!" We were shocked. Our friends had four kids of their own, so I couldn't imagine leaving them with three more. As my hand pushed the keys back across the table, my wife grabbed hold of them and said, "Thank you!" with perhaps the biggest smile I had ever seen. And that was that. We were off to Paris!

It was springtime, and it was glorious. The weather, the food, the wine—everything was perfect. Even the Mona Lisa smiled upon us. After ten years of madness, this was a dream come true. Our three days flew by as we indulged ourselves in every step and every moment. But there would be one final stop, L'Arc de Triomphe. In middle school French, this was my favorite landmark because I loved how it rolled off my tongue. We exited the metro, walked up the stairs, and there it was . . . behold, L'Arc de Triomphe! The textbooks didn't do it justice. The structure was massive, staking its personal claim as the heart of France. When I exclaimed "Wow!" my wife did as well. But she was staring in the opposite direction . . . down the Champs-Élysées, the famed luxury shopping district. She yanked my arm and yelled, "Let's go!" I never felt a tug so hard. She tugged me all the way to two gigantic letters, LV, marking the flagship store for Louis Vuitton. No wonder she was so agreeable to a final stop. As we entered, not one but two attendants approached, saying, "Bonjour." One escorted my wife to the left. The other guided me to the right. How did they know I wasn't interested in shopping? After miles of walking, it felt good to recline—aided by a tray full of mimosas. Sipping away, all I could say was, "Louis Vuitton," but this time with a smile. The strategy was brilliant. Three mimosas later, my wife returned, giddy with delight and two purses in hand. "Which do you like?" Was this a trick question? Would the Parisians take away my mimosa if I said, "Neither?" I tried to appear interested— touching, holding, admiring, casually searching for the price. Unzipping one, I looked inside and finally located the tag. I took a peek and gasped. There were four digits, all before the decimal. Every rational bone in my body wanted to shout, "Is Louis Vuitton out of his mind?"

In that moment, an inner battle ensued. I envisioned my up-and-down, all-around econ prof flailing his arms. How could anyone pay that much for these little handbags? *(Scarcity and total paralysis.)* Just because of their global brand? *(Monopoly.)* She'll probably bury them in the closet after a year *(sunk cost)*. We could cover the next two mortgage payments for this price *(opportunity cost)*. Don't let the fatigue and mimosas get to you *(diminishing returns)* . . . or the pressure of everyone standing there, watching you *(externalities).* Irrational, unthinkable, crazy . . . just say no!

—

Price weighed heavy for those few seconds, but the immeasurable also shined forth. What was four digits compared to the priceless opportunity of this anniversary moment? What data, stat, number, or graph could possibly outweigh the smile on her face right then? What quantifiable metric could have captured our past ten years? Ten years of her uprooting, being alone during deployments, raising three children, and packing time and again. Wasn't her selfless, sacrificial "brand" worth infinitely more? Despite the practical wisdom and valid concerns of positive economics, normative economics sharply intervened to remind me that price and value are not the same. The purse was a mere token, in fact an affordable bargain, to once again reaffirm and celebrate her infinite worth and priceless value on this momentous occasion. "What should be" perceived "what is" in its proper context. And suddenly, amid the chaos and confusion, standing before me was that perfectly linear, most rational straight-line decision.

As I looked into her eyes, I said, "The one on the left." She replied, "Not both?" I smiled. Embracing one positive, I pulled out the credit card and went normative. And later that night, it turned out to be the best economic decision ever.

—

Leaders, this is our daily battle: facing the scarcity and demands of each and every moment while trying to remember and fight for the normative. It's our calling to close the gap and connect the two worlds wherever and however we can. It's not easy, but the two don't conflict. Leadernomics is our reminder that economics has always been a social science, a leadership science, and a science that battles for humanity. "What is" is intended to serve "what should be." And when "what should be" is highly esteemed, "what is" can finally achieve the unimaginable. Transformative leadership isn't meant to be a daunting or confusing process, but a simple, linear journey, walked marginally, toward that equilibrium where "matter of fact" and "matter of priority" intimately meet. In leading others, it's here that the best, most worthy and maximizing investments will be discovered.

ACKNOWLEDGMENTS

To my wife, Grace: What can I say, honey? At every struggle and moment of doubt, you tweaked hope, catalyzed confidence, and shouted, "Go!" when I needed it most. And throughout, you helped me bring every principle to life. Most of all, thank you for always investing in others and living for eternal returns.

To Mom and Dad: *Sa-dang-hae-yo*. This book is my heart's gratitude to you. You gave up your story so that we might have ours. For us, your grandchildren, and every generation to follow, I say thank you.

To Samuel, Ellie, and Micah: Thank you for cheering Dad on and forbearing parental Leadernomics in the home. You three are my greatest gift and multiplier.

To my Chi-Hua-Hua faithfuls: Our rich friendship, all the laughter, and our priceless adventures in the faith have sustained me throughout this journey. Thank you.

To my Wellspring community and friends at The Park: For the thousand times you asked, "How's the book coming?" I can finally say, "It's done!" Thank you for always asking.

To Girl Friday Productions: Christina, you conveyed my vision better than I could articulate myself. Thank you for sharing my heart for *Leadernomics* and passing this baton with the greatest of care. From coach Marni (thank you!) to the finish line with my awesome production team (thank you, Kim and Alyssa!), GFP has been nothing short of impressive.

And last but not least, to all the young men and women faithfully serving our nation, today and tomorrow: With heartfelt gratitude, I SEE YOU. We need you. And we value your sacrifice and contribution. We owe you the best leaders possible . . . and not the next-best.

ABOUT THE AUTHOR

Seung Paik is a retired Air Force colonel who has been presenting Leadernomics for over twenty-five years. He has taught economics at the United States Air Force Academy and at the University of Colorado in Colorado Springs. He lives in San Francisco with his wife, Grace; his three children; and his little monster puppy, Lulu.